REVENGE

REVENGE

KEN FOXE

POOLBEG

Published 2010
by Poolbeg Books Ltd
123 Grange Hill, Baldoyle,
Dublin 13, Ireland
Email: poolbeg@poolbeg.com

© Ken Foxe 2010

The moral right of the author has been asserted.

Copyright for typesetting, layout, design
© Poolbeg Books Ltd

1 3 5 7 9 10 8 6 4 2

A catalogue record for this book is available from the British Library.

ISBN 978-1-84223-418-1

Typeset by Patricia Hope in Sabon 11.5/16
Printed by Litografia Rosés S.A., Spain

www.poolbeg.com

About the Author

Ken Foxe is the Public Affairs Correspondent with the *Sunday Tribune* and has been reporting on crime in Ireland for close to ten years. This is his first book. Visit www.kenfoxe.com.

Acknowledgements

A book like this would be simply impossible without the help of literally hundreds of people.

I would like to thank all of the gardaí who gave so much assistance to provide background material on the cases involved.

I would also like to thank the families who gave so willingly of their time to speak to me about their own tragedies.

I would also like to thank the many journalists who spoke to me about individual killings and provided valuable background information and assistance. No book like this would be possible without the extraordinary work done by the reporters who cover criminal trials and inquests. They provide an incredibly valuable repository of information for authors and for the historians of the future. They deserve much more credit than they get for their unerring accuracy.

In particular, I would like to thank my colleagues in the *Sunday Tribune*, especially News Editor Mick McCaffrey and Editor Noirín Hegarty, for giving me the time to complete a project like this. I would also like to thank colleagues Darren Boyle, Declan Power and Ron

Quinlan, all of my friends and the lads in St Brendan's GAA.

Thanks to my ever-supportive parents Mary and Michael Foxe and my brothers Greg, Damian and John.

Thanks to the Kehoe and Thompson families for their encouragement.

Most especially, thanks to my wonderful wife Brenda.

This book is dedicated particularly to the families in these cases who have yet to get closure and in the hope that those responsible for these killings will face justice.

Contents

Introduction

It is one of the most primitive of human motivations, a philosophy that dates all the way back to the Bible. "Life for life, eye for eye, tooth for tooth, hand for hand, foot for foot," says the Book of Exodus, outlining a barbaric system of summary "justice" that has never disappeared. The ageless pursuit of revenge has been a fixture of humanity, a constant throughout the world, no matter how "civilised" our society has become.

As far back as Julius Caesar, the Roman Emperor was murdered by a group of senators in revenge for having become simply too powerful. The famous Renaissance family of the Borgias were notorious too for being vengeful, routinely poisoning anybody who dared to cross them.

In culture, the motive of revenge is at the heart of many of Shakespeare's most famous plays, not least

Othello and *Hamlet*. From the canon of American literature, Herman Melville's *Moby Dick* is similarly concerned with a monomaniacal quest for vengeance as Captain Ahab pursues the great white whale that has "reaped" his leg. The phrases "revenge is sweet" or "revenge is a dish best served cold" seem invented for just such characters.

An entire film genre, the revenge movie, has developed around the pursuit of vengeance, the famous *Deathwish* movies the most obvious examples.

These celluloid and literary inventions are merely reflecting the world in which we live, a society where people are killed every day by someone who lives by that old biblical philosophy of an eye for an eye. Ireland is no different.

Since the turn of the millennium, nearly 600 people have lost their lives in violent incidents in this country and the spectre of homicide continues to haunt Irish society.

Murder, like all crime, conforms to a pattern. Certain people are most at danger: some obvious, some a little more surprising. Members of criminal gangs are at the greatest risk when it comes to murder in Ireland, shot dead for the most innocuous of reasons – the seizure of a drugs package, missing money or oftentimes the suspicion that they have been passing information to gardaí.

Men in their twenties living in the sprawling suburbs of Dublin or Limerick are also at risk, often victims of their own bravado and the over-consumption of drink or drugs. Amongst the new communities of immigrants, particularly those from Eastern Europe, there has also been a spike in crime.

Random murder, on the other hand, is still almost unheard of in Ireland, a few isolated incidents notwithstanding, and what at first may appear entirely random rarely turns out that way.

While men are five times more likely to be murdered than women, those women who die in violent incidents are very often killed by somebody they know: a husband, a jealous boyfriend, a former lover.

The murder of a child is always a particular tragedy but, despite public concerns over paedophile killers stalking the country, there simply is not the evidence to back up those fears. When children are killed, one of their parents has often been responsible.

Specific parts of the country are also most at risk of violent crime, particularly in the three main urban centres. In Dublin, areas where gang crime and drugs are rampant suffer worst, with the areas most affected being the Dublin West, Dublin North and Dublin South Central garda regions. Dublin West, a vast garda region covering Blanchardstown, Finglas, Cabra, Ballyfermot and Clondalkin, has seen more than fifty murders since the beginning of 2000.

The figures are stark and belie any suggestion that the crime problem in Ireland is simply exaggerated. During the 1960s, there was an average of just twelve people killed in violent incidents each year throughout the country. In 2002, by contrast, the Dublin South Central region alone, which covers the south inner city, recorded a total of fourteen separate killings in what proved a then record year for murder and violent death.

The year 2007 still holds the grim record for Ireland's worst ever crime year when a total of eighty-three violent killings were recorded by police but there are few detectives at work today who think that the Republic of Ireland won't ultimately outdo that sorry record.

Exact figures on who is carrying out the crime cannot be determined because many of the murders remain unsolved. However, based on the number of offenders going to prison for murder and manslaughter, the ratio of male to female killers is something in the region of fifteen to one.

What is most apparent is that many of those responsible are escaping justice and are unlikely to face prosecution. An analysis of crime figures in the first seven years of this century shows that at least 160 people have quite literally got away with murder and will never face prosecution. The garda conviction rate for violent deaths in that period stands at about forty per cent, although it is likely to rise as further cases come before the courts and new breakthroughs are made.

Some Irish counties are very fortunate and remain virtually murder-free. In County Mayo, there have been just four violent deaths recorded in the past eight years, including the notorious shooting of traveller John Ward by the farmer Padraig Nally.

Other counties with very low rates of violent death include Leitrim, Roscommon, east Galway, west Cork, Donegal, Sligo, north Cork and, not surprisingly, east Dublin, which covers many of the leafy suburbs on the southside of the capital.

The means by which people are dying have proved many and varied but around a quarter of all murders are carried out with firearms and a third with knives. The rest of the victims were killed by different means: beaten to death, strangled or, in one case, shot with a crossbow.

Determining exactly what has caused these crimes is a different tale altogether, but what links many of these violent killings is a simple motive: revenge.

That is where this book comes in, outlining twenty notorious Irish killings where the prime motivating factor was vengeance. In some cases, it has been blatant, where men – and it is almost invariably men – have set out on a mission of murder and mayhem, planning to avenge a perceived slight, a snub or, as has occasionally happened, another killing. Drawing on interviews with families, garda files and statements, court cases and inquests, twenty of the most famous Irish violent deaths are recounted here in detail.

There is the case of Michael Brady who, unbeknownst to himself, was signing his own death warrant when he strangled his wife Julie to death. Her brother Martin "Marlo" Hyland was a patient man and waited more than nine years before setting out on a mission to avenge his sister's killing. As Brady made his way home one evening after being released from prison, a motorbike rolled up beside him and he was shot dead. Detectives only ever had one suspect and that was Hyland, who was himself gunned down in 2006 as the garda net closed in on his massive criminal empire.

Then there was the case of Una Lynskey, who was abducted and killed, then dumped in the Dublin Mountains in 1971, setting in train a chain of tragedy which still continues to this day. Her brothers and a cousin – in a vengeful rage – kidnapped one of the men they believed responsible. As they tried to find out what had happened to Una, the unfortunate Martin Kerrigan was killed and they dumped him in the same spot their sister had been found.

Crimes of passion may seem on the face of it to be a different prospect; but, ultimately, they too are motivated by revenge.

There was the case of Sara Neligan, who planned to leave her lover Brian McBarron in 2007. When he found out, he was incandescent with rage and in his vengeful fury took her life to ensure that nobody else could have her. That case also highlights serious failings in the Irish justice system, as McBarron should have been in jail serving a sentence for a previous serious assault.

In other cases, scorned men – and women – have gone one step further, killing their own children in the ultimate revenge.

During September 2000, Stephen Byrne, a Kilkenny father, was suspicious that his wife was having an affair.

He killed her before driving himself and his two children off the pier at Duncannon, County Wexford. The sad deaths of his two children were amongst sixteen infanticides recorded in the space of just two years at the turn of the new millennium.

There are few in Ireland who are not aware of the Farah Swaleh Noor case, where the African immigrant was stabbed, then dismembered and dumped in the Royal Canal.

However, history was merely repeating itself. Four years earlier, the body of Romanian asylum-seeker Adrian Bestea had been discovered in the same stretch of the canal, stuffed inside a suitcase. Bestea had been killed after his girlfriend hired three hard men from the former USSR to "teach him a lesson" because he used to beat her. The men went too far and over the course of four hours beat him repeatedly, stopping only for breaks to drink vodka.

While something of a rare occurrence, women are more than capable of violent crime.

In 1993, seventeen-year-old Tracy Butler was stabbed to death in Limerick during a crime so ferocious that gardaí originally assumed that the two assailants were men. They weren't. The two attackers, Deborah Hannon and Suzanne Reddan, had carried out the assault in vengeance for the death of Hannon's father William. Tracy Butler had been a witness and was seen apparently laughing at the scene.

A motive as old as Ireland itself has been the notion of the informer. Ever since colonial days, the idea of assisting the British authorities has often been seen as the greatest crime an Irishman could commit.

Denis Donaldson, a high-ranking Sinn Féin official, committed just such a "crime". His murder in 2006, just three months after he was outed as a spy for British intelligence, remained unclaimed until 2009 when the Real IRA said they were responsible. The motive, although framed in their cold, clinical, militaristic language, was familiar enough – simple revenge for what they saw as cooperation with the Crown. The dividends of the peace process may well have been felt far and wide but for people like Denis Donaldson, it may be difficult to believe the conflict is over.

For the families of Joseph Rafferty and Paul Quinn, the forces of republicanism certainly do not appear to have gone away. The two men, murdered in 2005 and 2007 respectively, are both believed to have been killed by men with strong links to the IRA.

These twenty murders and violent killings present a snapshot of a changing Irish society, which moved from the policeman's paradise of the 1950s to a very much more dangerous world, beginning in the 1980s. Where once every murder had the capacity to shock, many killings now go virtually unremarked upon, meriting little more than a small story in the newspapers and broadcast bulletins of that day. Where once almost all killers were eventually prosecuted, now certain garda stations have up to a dozen open murder files, some with very little prospect of ever being solved.

REVENGE

These twenty killings, spanning close to half a century, chart the vastly changing landscape of crime in Ireland. They have taken place in different eras, across the rural and urban divide, involving people of every class, creed and age. What they all have in common is a single motive: revenge.

1

Dwayne Foster: The Death of Billy the Kid

Four years before Dwayne Foster died, the gardaí
issued a secret intelligence dossier about a crackdown
on armed raiders, which they called Operation Delivery.
Nineteen men were listed in the circular, effectively
showcasing a who's who of Irish crime, a mix of hardened
criminals and youngsters considered the up-and-
coming generation of Dublin gangland.

The nineteen were all suspected of involvement in a
series of cash-in-transit raids in 2002 and 2003. Their
modus operandi could not have been simpler: they
would swoop on security vans and hold one of the
workers at gunpoint. Cash from the back of the vehicle
would be handed out and the raiders would leave,
sometimes over a million euro richer.

Detectives right around the country were warned to
be on the alert, to learn the names and faces in the

bulletin so that if any of the men were ever stopped at a routine checkpoint or whilst acting suspiciously, they would not be allowed to walk away.

The men were all professional armed robbers, a *Reservoir Dogs*-style list of thieves, burglars, gunmen and getaway drivers, each with their own expertise and specialities.

Dwayne Foster – the self-styled "Billy the Kid" – was included on the list, a smiling portrait of a slightly awkward-looking young man grinning for the garda camera. In many ways, he seemed an unlikely criminal but he was already the chief suspect in a €1.3 million raid at Bettystown, County Meath, and at least two other raids. Foster was considered an expert shot, a rare commodity in Dublin gangland, where many assassinations fail because a gun jams or the killer simply misses his target.

Others in that list of nineteen were considered Ireland's best getaway drivers, dextrous in handling stolen cars or motorbikes, and evading any chasing gardaí. Some were simply organisers – skilled in spotting the weak links in bank security, identifying the chinks in their armour, recruiting inside men within financial institutions or security companies, who would then pass them information about when and where to strike.

More experienced criminals were also listed, including members of a gang known as the "Old Hands", a veteran group who were later responsible for a €270,000 "tiger" kidnapping in 2006. Despite the inclusion of the "Old Hands", no one on the list was much more than fifty years of age and all appeared to be in rude good health.

Within four years of that intelligence bulletin being issued, six of the nineteen men were already dead, including Dwayne "Billy the Kid" Foster.

His close friend Declan Curran, twenty-four, died in custody after an accidental drugs overdose while another, Anthony Spratt, thirty-four, took his own life in jail.

Curran was a notorious Dublin criminal, who had almost been put behind bars for life after he murdered a love rival, Willie O'Regan, in June of 2003. Gardaí had hoped to prosecute him and had built a strong case, only to see it collapse amidst strong suspicions of witness intimidation. When Curran died in November 2004, an autopsy showed traces of the anti-anxiety drugs Diazepam and Temazepam along with a dose of the painkiller codeine. Taken together, the prescription drugs proved a lethal cocktail. Detectives familiar with his rap sheet shed few tears for a man suspected of three murders; a man so deeply entrenched in gangland life that he always slept dressed in body armour.

Anthony Spratt, meanwhile, died four months after Curran. He killed himself in Mountjoy Prison, found hanged in his cell whilst serving a one-year sentence for road traffic offences. He was due for release within the month and some of his former associates do not believe that he could have committed suicide.

A fourth man on the list, twenty-three-year-old Paul Cunningham, was also dead, shot at his home in Blanchardstown, west Dublin, as part of a then-raging gang feud. Cunningham was asleep in an upstairs room of the house at the time when a gunman entered and finished his life. Nobody has been charged in connection with the murder.

Two other men from that part of the city – Shane Coates and Stephen Sugg, the so-called Westies – were also identified amongst the nineteen suspects and they too are now dead, believed to have been murdered after a drug deal went wrong in Spain. The two men were once considered amongst the leading criminals in Dublin, responsible for importing massive quantities of heroin, cocaine and cannabis in west Dublin. However, pressure from the gardaí finally began to tell and the two men relocated to what has become known as the Costa del Crime, the southern Spanish coast where dozens of Irish criminals still hide out.

In March 2006, Dwayne Foster was the sixth of the nineteen to perish, dead at just twenty-four years of age.

He had by that stage amassed twenty-eight convictions dating back to his teenage years and he was a key suspect in half-a-dozen armed raids. Foster's life of crime had begun like so many others, stealing and joyriding cars on the streets of Finglas, the west Dublin suburb that he called home. He grew up in the Valley Park estate there and in his late teens was already showing the violent rage and temper for which he will best be remembered. Once when he was eighteen, a garda patrol car came looking for him and drove towards his house. Foster appeared as if from nowhere and threw a concrete breeze block at the windscreen of the quickly reversing car.

As he grew up, he developed an expensive drugs habit, particularly for cocaine. But his addictions and out-of-control lifestyle proved costly and a few years before he died the criminal had been diagnosed with an aggressive but treatable cancer of the throat.

Detectives do not like to admit it but many of Dublin's criminals – even some of the most renowned – are prone to telling tales once in custody. In return for reduced charges or a positive word in court, they are often prepared to "rat" on others or offer up a drug seizure in exchange. Dwayne Foster was not like that. He vehemently despised the gardaí and when in custody would either pick a spot on the wall or verbally abuse them. In his latter years, gardaí never visited his home without the assistance of the heavily armed Emergency Response Unit as back-up.

Detectives had already fingered him for the €1.3 million Bettystown raid and he was the prime suspect for an armed hold-up of a security van at Lissenhall in Dublin, when €200,000 was stolen.

Officially listed on his criminal record is a conviction for robbery in December 1996 when he was sentenced to twenty-one months in prison. Three years later, he got another nine-month sentence for handling stolen goods and causing criminal damage. Most of his other convictions were for minor offences, particularly road traffic crimes, including drunken driving and failing to display insurance or tax. The May before he died, he was given a six-month sentence and disqualified from driving for eight years.

On 6 March 2006, Dwayne Foster was back in garda custody, this time on suspicion of murder. Detectives were jubilant, as it appeared that one of the country's most notorious criminals was finally going to get the type of prison sentence he deserved.

Not long after questioning began, Foster began to complain of feeling unwell at about 3.00 a.m. and was visited by a doctor shortly afterwards. Everything seemed to be in order and Foster went to sleep. A second doctor came to see him at 10.15 a.m. when he was prescribed medication, including the heroin substitute methadone.

Again, the suspect complained of feeling unwell and the second doctor was summoned again, this time at 8.00 p.m. He decided Foster should be taken to Beaumont Hospital where the prisoner was examined and subsequently discharged into the custody of the gardaí.

On his return to Coolock Garda station, he ate dinner, phoned his legal adviser and went to bed. At 2.00 a.m., a garda checked in on his cell and had a short conversation with him, the custody record shows. When the same garda returned to the cell half an hour later, he became concerned and tried to awaken him. The prisoner was "unresponsive" and an ambulance was called. There was blood around his mouth and nose.

Foster was taken back to Beaumont Hospital at around 3.00 a.m., where he was pronounced dead not long after. Deputy State Pathologist Dr Michael Curtis stated that the cause of death was as a result of intoxication with methadone. The time of death was given as 3.17 a.m.

Rewind forty-nine hours. A party was in full swing at Adare Green in Coolock. Edel Murtagh was celebrating her fortieth birthday and Donna Cleary was enjoying a rare night out, while her young son Clayton was at home being looked after by her parents Peter and Kathleen.

Dwayne Foster and three friends rolled up outside the house in a car and demanded to come in. Foster was known to many of the fifty or so people who gathered inside as a trouble-maker and Rhoda Flanagan, who owned the house, told them to leave.

Foster and his cronies had heard of the party at a function in the local GAA club earlier but had not been invited. They'd been seen injecting heroin and snorting cocaine at the club and nobody wanted to see them there.

The men picked up flower pots and began to smash them and throw them at the house. It was an infuriating act of pettiness but the celebrations – albeit in a more muted fashion – continued nonetheless. Allowing Dwayne Foster into the party would have been even worse, a guarantee of even more trouble from the baby-faced twenty-four-year-old criminal.

A further ten minutes passed and the silver Volvo car again cruised up outside the house just after 2.30 a.m. Dwayne Foster was inside, drunk and high – and vengeful, furious at what he perceived as a snub. The criminal who styled himself as "Billy the Kid" stepped out from the back seat of the car holding a Luger pistol. He fired indiscriminately towards the house, shooting off five rounds, two of which made it inside the house, the other three embedded in the walls.

The sound of bullets and shattering glass pierced the late night air. Amidst the mayhem, Donna Cleary slumped to the ground, hit once by Foster's wild firing.

"I saw the gunman get out. I could see the barrel of the gun. It was long and black. He was pointing it towards the house," said Rhoda Flanagan.

"I heard a bang and a shot. Every time he shot he moved his hands. After the third shot I was pushed to the ground."

Donna Cleary lay dying on the kitchen floor, begging to see her young son Clayton.

Edel Murtagh, whose birthday it was that night, explained the events to an inquest at the Dublin Coroner's Court.

"The car stopped at an angle and I saw a man jump from the rear door of the car," she said. "He had his hands together as if he was holding a gun. I heard a bang. I saw him fire a second shot and then I ran into the house.

"Everyone was screaming," she said. "I could see Donna's face. It was gaunt. I could see the life leaving her. She was bad. Her eyes were fixated."

Brian Lennon, another person at the party, went towards Donna Cleary as she lay on the ground, placing his coat beneath her head. "She was conscious and I spoke to her and said, 'Stay awake, stay awake' – and with that she slumped in my arms. I said 'Call an ambulance.' Donna was a great girl. She never took drink or drugs. We all loved her."

Garda Michael Leonard of Coolock Garda station was the first police officer to arrive at the scene. Donna Cleary was still alive, but her condition was rapidly deteriorating. "She spoke to me and she was very distraught," recounted the officer. "She was calling for her baby and she said she wanted to see her baby. I cleared the room as quickly as I could."

An ambulance arrived at the scene and Donna Cleary was rushed to the emergency unit at Beaumont Hospital.

At 4.26 a.m. she lost her fight for life.

She would never see her son Clayton again.

The post-mortem confirmed that she had died from a single gunshot wound, which had hit the right side of her chest. The round had entered her lung, causing shock and massive internal bleeding. The best efforts of medical personnel had been in vain and a massive cardiac arrest whilst on the operating table had finished her life.

Dwayne Foster, meanwhile, decided to lay low and travelled to a friend's house in the Curragh in County Kildare. At 11.00 p.m. on Sunday, he was arrested there along with two other friends, two associates who both also featured on the Operation Delivery dossier. The owner of the house in the Curragh and his wife were also taken into garda custody.

Detectives suspected that Foster had showered and changed his clothes in the meantime. He had also disposed of the weapon, and it has never been recovered.

As the chief suspect arrived in custody, it became clear to detectives that he should already have been in prison. In May 2006, Foster had been sentenced to three months in prison for road traffic offences. He had appealed the conviction but when the hearing came up for review, he was not in court and the appeal was dismissed. However, the gardaí had never received the warrant and were unable to act upon it.

Irrespective of that, two other bench warrants for his arrest had also been issued a month before Donna Cleary died, for driving without insurance. Dwayne Foster most certainly would have been in custody had gardaí been able to find him before that night in Coolock.

The then Garda Commissioner Noel Conroy was forced to defend his organisation as opposition politicians said Ms Cleary's murder represented a "new low" in Irish crime. Commissioner Conroy said: "When you look at the number of people that were involved in trying to locate him for the crime that we suspected him for, it took a lot of man hours. You're talking about anything in the region of fifty personnel searching for that individual and that was the difficulty we were faced with at the time."

As Dwayne Foster was led through the door of Coolock Garda station, gardaí were optimistic – for once – that Dwayne Foster would be charged with murder. Three witnesses, all of whom knew the suspect previously, had identified him from the scene. Gardaí warned them that they might face threats of intimidation but all insisted they would give evidence.

Within a few hours Dwayne Foster fell ill and within twenty-four hours, he was dead. Gardaí could not press charges against a dead man and his three "accomplices" were all effectively in the clear. Detectives prepared a file for the Director of Public Prosecutions but even before it was sent, they feared that they had drawn the losing hand. Proving the men were with Dwayne Foster on the night in question would have been easy; proving they knew he had a gun or what he intended to do was more complicated.

For the family of Donna Cleary, all talk of a "new low" is hollow. There had been so many lows before Donna's death and so many since that any faith they had in the justice system is long since gone.

Every time an innocent victim is caught up in gangland crime, the government of the day promises that this will be the "final straw", that this will be the killing which will mark an end to the spiral of violence that has afflicted Irish society these past two decades.

The first "new low" was probably the murder of Veronica Guerin, the crime reporter with the *Sunday Independent*. Her killing sparked genuine change, with a major overhaul of antiquated legislation and the introduction of the Criminal Assets Bureau. The Hollywood version of her life, the film directed by Joel Schumacher, boasts in its postscript a major reduction in crime following her death, as if Ireland had somehow ushered in a new era of peace and tranquillity in response to her death. The reality, of course, bore no resemblance to that celluloid world, as drugs in actual fact became ever more freely available and life on the streets even cheaper.

"New low" followed "new low" as innocent bystanders inevitably ended up being caught in the wrong place at the wrong time, mistaken for drug dealers or simply shot dead because they witnessed a gangland crime. Donna Cleary's father Peter has seen and heard of so many "new lows" that he can scarcely remember them all.

There was Brian Fitzgerald, the Limerick doorman who was shot dead because he refused to allow drugs to be sold inside the nightclub where he worked. His murder in 2002 by a major Limerick criminal gang sparked a deluge of talk – and yet more talk – from Irish politicians, who promised this would be the final straw.

Six years later, things had improved not one iota in Limerick when Shane Geoghegan, a rugby-mad twenty-eight-year-old, was shot dead because he bore a slight resemblance to the intended target of a gangland assassination.

Fast forward another six months and another innocent man lay dead. Roy Collins was shot dead in the family-owned amusement arcade in the city because his cousin had given evidence against a gangland criminal.

That was just in Limerick.

In Dublin, there was Baiba Saulite, the young Latvian mother who was shot dead on her own front doorstep while she was talking to a friend. A north Dublin crime syndicate was suspected of carrying out the murder as a favour for another criminal.

The same gang was also responsible for shooting Anthony Campbell, a plumber who happened to be working at a house where gangster Martin "Marlo" Hyland was staying. He died because he was a potential witness.

All of these crimes were "watersheds", moments when the nation was supposed to be standing at a precipice; where the choice was either standing up to gangland crime or falling over the edge.

Over the edge we went.

"Every time it happens, all we ever hear are these same things, a watershed, that the person was in the wrong place at the wrong time," said Donna's father Peter. "How can you say something like that? You're at a house party and you are in the wrong place at the wrong time. Where is the right place? Does that mean that every kid doesn't ever go to a party again because they might be in the wrong place? Should we all just stay at home and never leave?

"The politicians go into the Dáil, they roar and scream all day but it doesn't stop innocent people getting killed outside. They should do something about the law of the land instead of making speeches."

In the aftermath of Dwayne Foster's death, it seemed possible that somebody would still be prosecuted in connection with the Donna Cleary murder.

After all, his three accomplices had travelled back with him and one of them at least must have been the getaway driver. More than a dozen witnesses had placed them at the scene and some had picked them out of a line-up.

Peter Cleary said: "What sort of a justice system do we have when you cannot be prosecuted when you are there when a murder is committed and you know what happened? If it was a politician's daughter or son who was killed, there would have been more than just uproar. With the evidence against these men, they would have been brought before the court but what we have is a law for one and a law for the other. At the very least, they should have

23

been brought to court to let the jury decide if they are innocent or guilty. You look at the Veronica Guerin case and there were no eyewitnesses there and yet the people involved were all brought before the courts, whether they were the ones who shot her or not."

For the Cleary family, the confirmation of a decision that no prosecution would be made came as another shock on the day they found out exactly how their daughter had died.

"We got absolutely nothing from the DPP," explained Peter, "not even the courtesy of a phone call or a letter. The people of this country pay their wages but they are answerable to nobody."

However, the Cleary family is determined that their daughter's death will not be forgotten, that the memory of it will not dissipate and dwindle any further as new murders consume the public and Donna's death becomes just another statistic.

"As long as I'm living, I'll never let this die," said Peter. "The attitude in this country is to pass the buck, then sweep it under the carpet and forget all about it. But as long as I have breath, I will slate the government for the lack of protection they provide to people.

"There were three bench warrants out for Dwayne Foster's arrest. If they had been acted upon, he would have been in prison. All four of them that night were known to be dangerous criminals. They all have rap sheets the length of the road, never mind your arm, yet they were walking the streets that night.

"There were five or six shots fired when Donna died and we could have been burying five or six kids in the week that followed."

Life goes on in the Cleary household and Donna's parents have become a de facto mother and father to Clayton, who still asks for his real mum all the time.

"I have to do part-time work and Kathleen has to as well so we can look after the little fella. We work, we collect him from school, we look after him and that's basically our life now because of that toe-rag," said Peter. "The little fella still looks for her. Then he asks, 'Did a bold man kill my mammy?' All we can say is yes. When I'm out and I see a blonde girl, I get the feeling that it is Donna. I still expect her to come through the door. Our whole lives are just torn apart.

"It doesn't get any easier. People say time is a great healer but it isn't. If you lose a son or daughter, then you'll know what I mean. Around Christmas time when the little fella is wondering where his mammy is; that's the most difficult part. What are you supposed to tell him?"

2.

Denis Donaldson: Dead Man Walking

All Denis Donaldson wanted as his life drew to a close was some "peace and quiet".

The IRA double agent had moved to a pre-Famine-era cottage in the wilds of County Donegal where he lived without central heating or even running water. At night, he would read by the light of an old oil lamp and to warm himself he chopped wood and placed it on the fire at the centre of his living room. He drew water from a nearby well, which he stored and used for washing and cooking.

He knew nobody locally and lived a hermitical life, only ever leaving the house on short visits to a nearby town to collect provisions. The so-called super-spy looked a shadow of his former self, sporting an unkempt beard and wearing worn-out combat trousers and an old navy blue shirt.

It was a far cry from his days in the corridors of power in Stormont, where he wore sharp suits and passed information on his Sinn Féin and IRA comrades to both MI5 and the Police Service of Northern Ireland.

In December 2005, he had been outed as a spy by Sinn Féin President Gerry Adams and in a statement read out to RTÉ had admitted he had been working as a mole.

From that moment, Denis Donaldson was a dead man walking.

He left behind his life in Belfast and moved to his secret bolthole in the wilds of County Donegal. Denis Donaldson might have hoped he could just go, just disappear, but he was hardly forgotten.

Sunday World journalist Hugh Jordan recalled meeting a source in March of 2006, who in the course of a conversation about other things speculated that Donaldson might be hiding out in County Donegal. Jordan said: "I was having a cup of tea with this contact and they said, 'Do you know who has a house in Donegal?' I asked who? He said, 'I would put money on that's where Denis Donaldson is.'"

The information was vague but it was enough to convince Jordan that a trip west from his newspaper's offices in Belfast was more than worthwhile.

He explained: "I went to Gweedore on Monday morning and to be honest, without an enormous amount of difficulty, two days later I found him about seven or eight miles outside Glenties.

"I drove back to Belfast that night and arranged to do some 'sneaky' filming and come back early in the morning. Myself and a friend drove past the house and came back. It was a wee pre-Famine house, very basic type of place."

Hugh Jordan approached the house with both of his hands held out in front of him. He didn't know if Denis Donaldson would recognise him and the Sinn Féin mole had more than legitimate reasons to fear for his own safety. "He came to the door and closed it behind him," said Jordan. "He could see me. I waved to him and he waved back. I said 'Hello, Denis' and explained who I was. He said he knew who I was.

"We had this bizarre conversation where he said he was not doing any interviews. I was refusing to go and he was just too polite to tell me to leave. It was a stilted conversation; I would ask, 'How are you getting on?' then 'Why did you do it?' He would either refuse to answer or give me something very vague. At any time, I was expecting him to walk away but we got fourteen minutes off him."

Donaldson spoke briefly about his arrest in 2002 when he was accused of being the key figure in a Sinn Féin spying ring at Stormont, the seat of government in Northern Ireland. In the aftermath of what came to be known as Stormontgate, the devolved government in Northern Ireland collapsed.

Denis Donaldson claimed that he had been thrown to the wolves by his handlers in the British secret service. It was their plan to prop up the moderate UUP leader David Trimble in the face of strong opposition from the Democratic Unionist Party (DUP) and its charismatic leader Ian Paisley.

Donaldson explained his conspiracy theory to Hugh Jordan in the final interview that he gave.

Donaldson said: "It was for whatever agenda they were up to – and that agenda is all too obvious. The plan was to collapse the institutions to save Trimble – David Trimble was trying to out-DUP the DUP and in the end the DUP swallowed him up. The whole idea was to get Trimble off the hook and get republicans the blame. But it didn't work, because Trimble is history now."

Denis Donaldson would not be drawn any further on what had happened, though; why a one-time friend of hunger striker Bobby Sands would turn to the other side and betray his friends.

"How did you manage to find this place?" he asked Hugh Jordan. "You don't see much of anyone here, not even the gardaí. They've been up and down past here, but they never came in. I'm not hiding, though. I just want to be left alone. I don't go anywhere."

After less than quarter of an hour, Hugh Jordan left, knowing there was nothing more to be gained from staying around.

"I always remember he said something like, 'I just want peace and quiet,'" recalls Jordan. "Then he said, 'I don't suppose there'll be any peace now.'

"I shook his hand and I left. We went up the road, checked the film and we had it. I rang my editor Colm McGinty and told him what we had got. He said: 'You're joking, how did you manage that?' I drove back to Belfast and wrote the story. We made a famous TV ad, and it was the first time we had ever used moving pictures for one of our adverts.

"The gardaí knew he was there but he wouldn't talk to anybody. Other reporters called to the house but he wouldn't even come out.

"It was as though he had been banished to await his fate. Three weeks later, he was dead."

Denis Donaldson was born in the staunchly Catholic Short Strand area of Belfast in 1950. By the time he was in his teens, he was already exhibiting strong republican sympathies and had joined the movement before the Troubles had even broken out.

At age twenty, Donaldson had his first serious run-in with the law when he was caught planting a bomb in a distillery in Belfast. He was sentenced to four years in jail, the only spell he ever served behind bars. Whilst in prison, he became a close friend of Bobby Sands and a famous photograph of the two men, arms slung over each other's shoulders, is one of only a handful of pictures taken of the hunger striker in prison before his death.

On his release from jail, Denis Donaldson quickly became a key figure in the IRA, and a trusted lieutenant of Gerry Adams, who was starting to wrest control of the organisation from the old guard in the south which until then had dominated. Donaldson was particularly important in building up links with foreign terrorist and revolutionary groups, which would provide arms and training to the IRA at key times.

In August 1981, Donaldson and a leading IRA gunrunner were arrested by police at the airport in Orly, south of Paris. The two men had travelled using forged papers and admitted they had been at a training camp in Lebanon for several months. Donaldson was allowed to return home and was not prosecuted.

Donaldson also forged links with other terrorist groups including the Basque separatist grouping ETA and the Palestine Liberation Organization. He was also involved in cultivating contacts for the IRA in the corridors of power of Washington DC.

In 1983, he unsuccessfully stood in local council elections and at some time around this period he was first turned by the British security services after, as Donaldson put it later, "compromising myself". A story from the time suggests that he had been caught in bed with a local woman but his wife Alice already knew about it so the affair seems unlikely to have been the literal turning point. There were dozens of other rumours, of other indiscretions, of a "shoplifting" incident in Marks & Spencer, but none of them seemed sufficient to turn a man into a traitor.

Donaldson would have been a pivotal person in the armoury of British intelligence, with knowledge about the leadership of the IRA, its international contacts and, crucially, importation of weapons into Ireland.

He became a key backroom man in Sinn Féin as the party made its first tentative steps towards a political solution in the North, leading to the first IRA ceasefire in 1994. Donaldson also continued globe-trotting on behalf of the organisation, at one stage travelling to Lebanon in an attempt to have the Beirut hostage Brian Keenan freed from captivity. Denis Donaldson met with senior figures from Hizbullah but to no avail. Brian Keenan later recalled: "For the whole period of my incarceration, only two human beings put their lives at risk on my behalf – one was Terry Waite and the other was Denis Donaldson."

Donaldson was then moved to the United States, where he helped pave the way for visits to the US capital by Martin McGuinness and Gerry Adams.

By 2002, British intelligence had recruited another mole inside Sinn Féin, somebody not as highly ranked as Donaldson, but who was similarly well-placed. The new informant revealed that Donaldson, by now the head of the party's administration, was believed to have been at the heart of a Sinn Féin spying ring in Stormont, something which Donaldson had neglected to mention to his handlers.

On 4 October, Donaldson and two other men were arrested on suspicion of intelligence-gathering. Two computer disks were removed from Sinn Féin offices in Stormont while thousands of sensitive documents were also reported to have been discovered during a raid on Donaldson's Belfast home. Two days after the raid, Donaldson appeared in court, charged with five offences including providing information that could be used for the purposes of terrorism. Eight days after that, the devolved government in Northern Ireland collapsed.

Three years later, all charges against the three men were dropped without explanation at a court hearing when police were not granted a public interest immunity certificate, which would have protected the identity of the second informant. The court was told the Director of Public Prosecutions would not now be continuing with the case because it was "no longer in the public interest".

Donaldson's days as a British spy were numbered. He was summoned to a meeting with his handlers and told that Sinn Féin were close to finding out about his secret activity. Protection and the possibility of a new life abroad under an assumed name were offered. Donaldson, however, decided he would take his chances.

At a hastily arranged press conference, Sinn Féin President Gerry Adams disclosed that the party had an informer in its ranks and that his name was Denis Donaldson. He had been suspended by the party following his admission that he was a spy.

Gerry Adams said: "You'll know that our party has expelled Denis Donaldson, who is a long-standing member, after we uncovered and he admitted that he was working as a British agent. Denis Donaldson was approached by the PSNI and he was told that his life was in danger, that he was going to be outed as an agent and an informer.

"This was brought to my attention the day after it happened because Denis Donaldson went to [an official] . . . and said to him the police were at my door, they told me my life was in danger, and he was advised to get in touch with his solicitor.

"He was interviewed in the Sinn Féin office at the Falls Road in Belfast. He admitted working for the British as an agent."

At a Dublin hotel, Denis Donaldson and his solicitor agreed to meet with the RTÉ reporter Charlie Bird, who travelled to meet them, expecting an interview with the super-spy, but instead listened as an "extremely nervous" Denis Donaldson read out a short prepared statement.

The bespectacled informer began: "My name is Denis Donaldson. I worked as a Sinn Féin assembly group administrator at parliament buildings at the time of the PSNI raid on the Sinn Féin offices in October 2002, the so-called Stormontgate affair.

"I was a British agent at the time. I was recruited in the 1980s after compromising myself during a vulnerable time in my life. Since then, I have worked for British intelligence and the RUC/PSNI Special Branch.

"Over that period, I was paid money. My last two contacts with Special Branch were as follows: two days before my arrest in October 2002 and last night, when a member of the Special Branch contacted me to arrange a meeting.

"I was not involved in any republican spy ring in Stormont. The so-called Stormontgate affair was a scam and a fiction, it never existed. It was created by Special Branch.

"I deeply regret my activities with British intelligence and the RUC/PSNI Special Branch. I apologise to anyone who has suffered as a result of my activities, as well as to my former comrades and especially to my family, who have become victims in all of this."

From there, Denis Donaldson tried to drift into obscurity, moving into the family-owned cottage near Glenties in County Donegal. He lived a simple life, eschewing all of his former comforts but more importantly refusing any police protection, despite the sure knowledge that his life was under threat.

Denis Donaldson remained anonymous until that March morning when Hugh Jordan of the *Sunday World* came calling, giving the final public statement that would ever be made about his remarkable life.

On Monday, 3 April, two republican renegades made that same trip the seven or eight miles from the village of Glenties to the isolated cottage that Denis Donaldson now called home. They came towards the house, armed with a shotgun, some time that evening. Denis Donaldson, it seems, knew somebody was coming and attempted to bolt his front door. The killers used a sledge hammer to break through the door.

The assassins, hell-bent on revenge on the informer, entered the house. Denis Donaldson did not shout or scream and knew the inevitable had come at last. They shot at him at least four times, twice through the door and twice more when they got inside.

Within hours, the IRA issued a statement saying they had not been responsible. The letter, signed with their *nom de guerre* of P. O'Neill, said: "The IRA had no involvement whatsoever in the death of Denis Donaldson."

Sinn Féin leader Gerry Adams also condemned the shooting, saying he wanted to disassociate the republican community from the men who had carried out the callous attack. "We are all living in a different era," said Adams. "Some of us are trying very, very hard to build a future and one in which everybody will have a share. Those who carried out the killings have no interest in that."

Early rumours that Donaldson may have committed suicide were also quickly put to rest. Then Minister for Justice Michael McDowell made an unusual statement in which he disclosed that Donaldson had been shot in the head and that his right forearm was almost severed in the attack.

"Gardaí are working on the theory that it is not a suicide, it is a homicide," said McDowell.

Officers quickly sealed off all roads leading towards the cottage as a technical and forensic examination of the scene took place. Gardaí admitted they had been "in close communication" with Denis Donaldson in the months leading up to his death.

Chief Superintendent Terry McGinn said they had made contact with him in January: "We made ourselves known to Mr Donaldson, we introduced ourselves, we offered him our facilities here in terms of whatever protection he needed and we have been in close communication with him."

She said garda patrols routinely drove by the cottage to check that nothing untoward had happened.

Officers had actually seen him just twenty-four hours before he died in Glenties at around 5.00 p.m. A member of the public had also spotted him early the following morning, but they may have been mistaken.

But the "close communication" between the gardaí and Denis Donaldson yielded little in the way of clues.

Any number of theories were expounded upon. Would the IRA risk shooting him or could they be seen to allow an informer of such standing to just carry on? Was a dissident republican group responsible, perhaps, trying to appeal to Sinn Féin supporters who believed the IRA had gone soft on people who had cooperated with the British security services? Other less likely theories also emerged of British intelligence silencing a man who knew too much or a loyalist group trying to sow seeds of difficulty for a republican movement that had come in from the cold.

Gardaí were remaining – at least publicly – tight-lipped, as usual. Asked whether republicans were involved in the killing, Chief Superintendent Terry McGinn would only say: "At this stage, I am keeping an open mind on the inquiry and following all avenues."

The murder was carefully planned. It was clear the killer – or killers – knew the exact location of the cottage. They had probably driven by before and knew Donaldson's movements. They had used a shotgun, knowing it would prove difficult to do a ballistics trace on it.

This was a murder of national significance and even sparked a response from the then-Taoiseach Bertie Ahern, who was forced to admit that no progress had been made. "We have no intelligence, no information, to indicate whether . . . it is in retribution for some past event or some falling out along the way or whether it is some dissident group. We don't know and we will do everything we can to try and find that out. It is important to do so in any murder."

Donaldson's family then went public, saying they believed the IRA's denial that it had any involvement and asking that the murder not be used for political point-scoring.

"Denis was a loving husband, a devoted father and grandfather and a good brother," they said. "The events of recent months have been very difficult for our family. In December, Denis left his home in Belfast and moved to Donegal where it was his desire that he be left alone to rebuild his life."

On Saturday, 4 April, the super-spy was buried at the City Cemetery, following a low-key church ceremony in West Belfast. The gardaí had still made no progress.

A year later and they were no closer to catching his killer, issuing an anniversary appeal for witnesses to come forward. Nobody came forward.

Six months further on and there was still no news – only the revelation that Donaldson's family had now been forced to make a complaint to the Garda Ombudsman about the way in which the case was being handled. They said gardaí had not given advance warning to Denis Donaldson about threats to his life and raised questions about the possibility that the cottage near Glenties was being bugged at the time of the murder. Sinn Féin President Gerry Adams had also written to the Minister for Justice on their behalf, raising their concerns.

An inquest into the death was repeatedly delayed, ostensibly because the garda investigation was still ongoing. However, the Donaldson family wanted it to proceed, believing that the garda probe was likely to "go nowhere".

And nowhere it continued to go.

The case remained cold until April 2009 when the Real IRA – the splinter group behind the bombing of Omagh – finally claimed responsibility.

They had just murdered two soldiers at the Massereene Barracks in County Antrim and were now willing to claim the murder of Denis Donaldson.

In a chilling interview given to Suzanne Breen of the *Sunday Tribune*, a representative of the RIRA said they had long debated whether or not to kill Denis Donaldson. "Some individuals thought it was better propaganda value keeping him alive because it increased Provisionals' [IRA] dissatisfaction with their leadership," he said. "They were angry at Donaldson's treachery and angry at their leadership for not executing him, for letting him slip off to Donegal unharmed.

"But the other argument put forward among our leadership was that by executing Donaldson, we could show – unlike the Provos – that we weren't prepared to tolerate traitors. We would prove that while the Provos shirked their duty . . . true and faithful republicans would not."

Donaldson never said a word as they broke into his house, the Real IRA spokesman said, as if he was simply resigned to what was about to happen. "The look on his face wasn't even one of shock. He seemed to know what was coming."

Denis Donaldson had no means of protecting himself, no handgun, not even a "baseball or hurley bat". He simply knew that when his killers came calling, fighting back would prove useless.

"He just ran into the back room. There was a struggle, and he ended up on the ground. He didn't cry out or plead for mercy. He remained silent all the time," said the Real IRA man.

Donaldson's lower right arm had been practically blown off during the attack, a symbolic gesture – some suggested – because he had taken payment to work as an informer. The truth was much more mundane. He had simply raised his hand in a self-protective instinct.

They did not feel the need to torture him as dozens of other suspected informers had been in the past. "There was no need to debrief him," the Real IRA spokesman explained in the cold clinical language of the soldier. "He had done no damage to our organisation."

Asked whether they feared arrest or prosecution for what they had done, they could not have been any more dismissive.

"We don't believe it's going anywhere. They haven't a clue. Only a dozen people knew we executed Donaldson – our Army Council and the volunteers involved.

"We always intended to claim the operation but we wanted to wait until we had first executed Crown force personnel. That was secured at Massereene. The time is particularly right now, when we're being accused of treachery by others, to show what we do to traitors."

3

Paul Quinn: They Have Not Gone Away

When they buried Paul Quinn, they could not even fold his arms and hands across the body, as if in prayer. Every single bone in his body had been broken and, try as the undertakers might, there was no way to hold his pulped hands in that position.

Twenty-one-year-old Paul Quinn had been lured across the border from his home in Cullyhanna, County Armagh, with the promise of work. It was a set-up and a gang of men lay in wait, dressed in boiler suits and masks, armed with iron bars, bats and sticks, some studded with nails.

It was claimed that the "dogs on the streets" of South Armagh knew that Quinn had fallen victim to a criminal feud and that he was, supposedly, up to his neck in fuel smuggling and other racketeering.

Two years earlier, twenty-eight-year-old Joseph Rafferty – a self-employed courier – was shot dead outside his west Dublin apartment in a killing that bore every hallmark of a professional assassination.

Suspicion almost immediately moved towards the possibility of a criminal background, a suggestion by certain quarters that Joe Rafferty had diced with drug dealers.

The two cases – separated by two years, and in two very different parts of Ireland – would appear at first glance to have little or nothing in common: two men who lived by the sword dying by that sword.

The truth, however, could not have been more different.

Paul Quinn was no master criminal. As his own father Stephen put it, he didn't have "tuppence" to his name on the day that he died. Joseph Rafferty was not a criminal either; simply a man unfortunate enough to have caused offence to a young "hard man" with links to the IRA.

Both men were murdered by the IRA, an organisation that keeps pretending it has gone away, but time and time again raises its head above the parapet to commit "peace-time" atrocities.

Joseph Rafferty's offence could not have been more mundane: he was too good-looking. A local thug's girlfriend had taken a shine to him and the jealous republican harboured a serious grudge. For six months, the IRA hoodlums told Joe Rafferty they would get him. Eventually, they did.

Paul Quinn's "crime" was that he didn't respect the IRA. The organisation that had ruled the streets of South Armagh for more than thirty years was beginning to lose its steely grip. A young republican – who was a member of a prominent IRA family – did not like Paul Quinn. The two men had tangled on two, perhaps three, different occasions. Every time, Paul Quinn had bested his adversary.

After that, he was warned to leave Cullyhanna, told that his days were numbered if he continued to live in his own home town. He refused to bow down, refused to leave the family home or his girlfriend Emma Murphy. For that, it seems, he had to die – for there can be no brooking of dissent when it comes to the IRA.

Quinn had made a fool of the young republican, the son of the OC (Officer Commanding) of the IRA in South Armagh. He had punched and kicked him during an altercation and came out the better of it.

A week or two later, Paul Quinn was confronted in a bar and another fight broke out. This time, two brothers – the sons of another prominent republican – tried to take him on. Paul Quinn made fools of them as well.

From there, it is mere speculation as to exactly what happened. Some say a meeting of the local IRA leadership decided that the young Cullyhanna man had to be taught a lesson. Others believe that it was more informal than that, simply an arrangement by the group of young republicans to administer their standard form of punishment, one that they had been brought up to believe in.

For at least two weeks before Paul Quinn was murdered, he and three of his friends were kept under close surveillance. The IRA gang plotted out their likely movements and whereabouts, where they liked to socialise, who they hung around with. Trying to kidnap Paul Quinn directly would probably prove difficult as he was already on his guard and, in a direct fist-fight, he had already shown them who was boss on a number of occasions.

The IRA gang decided on a location, finding a little-used cowshed just south of the border in County Monaghan. Two of Paul Quinn's friends were working there and the gang took them to the byre, where they began to torture them and told them to phone Paul Quinn. They beat one of the friends repeatedly, hitting him and eventually breaking his leg. He would not give in, could not give up his friend. They started on the second friend, pounding him with their fists and bats. They threatened to mutilate him and break his bones. The agony became too much for him and he phoned Paul Quinn, telling him there was work across the border if he was available. As he spoke, the men stood above him, ready to pounce if he let his guard down for a second, if he let anything slip about what was about to happen.

Paul Quinn had no full-time job; he effectively lived hand-to-mouth, eking out an existence from week to week, picking up a bit of driving work here and a bit of farming work there to make a meagre income. The twenty-one-year-old was delighted with the offer of work. He called a friend and told him there was work clearing the shed if he wanted it. The two men drove across the border to Oram, laughing and joking as they drove, not an idea of what lay in store for them. They drove into the yard and stood there chatting for a few minutes.

A man came running towards them. Paul Quinn tried to flee but it was too late.

There were twelve or thirteen of them there, all dressed in boiler suits and surgical gloves, well-prepared for the task at hand. Whatever crime they planned to commit that day, they would leave no trace.

They had armed themselves with an array of weaponry; iron bars and sticks studded with spikes and nails. They took Paul Quinn away from his friends.

They beat him, and then beat him again, and beat him until every major bone in his body was broken. If they didn't intend to kill him when they began, it was surely their intention by the time the attack finished half an hour later. On his lower body they used the iron bars, raining down blow after blow, beating him literally to a pulp. For his upper body and head, they used the sticks, embedded with nails.

His friends were forced to listen to the horrific thud of iron on bone, time after time. At first, Paul Quinn's screams were all that could be heard. But as the blows came thick and fast, his impassioned pleas for help and mercy became ever fainter.

"You know who the bosses around here are now," they said. "We are the bosses."

As they drove away in a van, they sprayed some unknown disinfectant around the cowshed, presumably a chemical that would help cleanse the crime scene.

Whatever chance Paul Quinn might have had of surviving, they were also intent on snuffing that out. They took the phones from all four men and smashed them. One of them – purely by accident – remained working and they managed to ring Paul's girlfriend Emma Murphy, who came to the scene as quickly as she could. When she arrived at the farmyard, the others tried to keep her away from Paul, wanting to spare her the horror.

She found her boyfriend barely conscious. Paul asked her if she could bring him home but he began to drift away and his speech became incoherent. In an interview with the *Irish Mail on Sunday* at the time, she described those final moments, of how Paul's friend Brendan Nugent rang and said: "Call an ambulance."

"He didn't really open his eyes much," she said. "He was just more or less moaning and screaming with the pain. He was in a bad way. I thought first that he had got bullet shots in his legs but it wasn't bullet shots, it was actually the bone sticking out of his knee.

"Then he kept telling me to take him home and I kept telling him I couldn't take him home, that there was an ambulance coming. He kept asking when was the ambulance coming but he couldn't even say the sentences right. He just kept muttering."

Paul Quinn slipped into unconsciousness in the ambulance *en route* to hospital and never woke again. He arrived at the Lourdes Hospital in Drogheda, County Louth, where he was pronounced dead at 8.00 p.m. that Saturday evening.

The clay on Paul Quinn's grave had barely settled when Sinn Féin proclaimed themselves and their military wing, the IRA, innocent of any crime.

Local MP Conor Murphy said: "There are wild and baseless allegations being made. However, I do not believe there is any republican involvement in this murder."

Sinn Féin President Gerry Adams went even further, going so far as to suggest that the murder was the result of a feud over the lucrative fuel smuggling trade that thrives along the border between the Republic and the North. "The people involved are criminals," he said. "They need to be brought to justice and it is fairly obvious to me that it is linked to fuel smuggling and to criminal activity."

The mealy-mouthed words of Sinn Féin, however, were simply a lie, shot down by the Independent Monitoring Commission the following month when they confirmed there had been IRA involvement in the death. PSNI Chief Constable Hugh Orde also said it was impossible to say whether there had been a sanctioned plot to abduct and murder Paul Quinn but that there was a probable republican connection.

"People who were associated with the IRA at some stage were definitely involved in that crime," he said. "That does not mean in any way shape or form that this was an authorised event . . . I think that's a totally different debate."

Seventeen arrests later and gardaí tasked with investigating the brutal crime in County Monaghan on 20 October 2007 are no closer to pressing charges.

Paul Quinn's father Stephen and mother Briege will not give up, however, knowing that there are people out there who can solve their son's brutal murder but are simply too afraid to come forward. Every day, Stephen Quinn walks the streets of Cullyhanna and comes face to face with the men he believes killed his son.

"I do see them, nearly every day, I suppose," he says. "It's hard, you do it and you pass no remarks, just keep going and don't let them see it in you. That's about all you can do. You can't say anything, do anything else. You just have to leave it to the gardaí or the PSNI."

The gang responsible for murdering Paul Quinn has openly intimidated potential witnesses, telling them that they will be next if they agree to testify. Gardaí have disclosed that one potential witness has already been warned that there is a threat against his life.

Stephen Quinn, though, does not fear them, for what more can they do to him?

"They can't do much more to me," he said. "They can kill me as well if they want. As the fella says, my

49

life is not worth a whole lot anyway after what they done. They made out and said it was criminals, fighting amongst each other. But it was all about Paul, he beat a fella and his father was high up in the IRA. He gave another boy a bit of a fight. This young boy, he would have picked a row twice or three times and every time he did, Paul beat him."

After one altercation, a family member came out to Quinn and vowed that he would be killed and "found in a black bag on the road".

"That's what really happened to Paul," explained Stephen Quinn. "He wasn't afraid of them sort of boyos. They could not see somebody stand up to them because that was bad in their eyes. There were a few boys in this area who stood up to them, who had no respect for them whatsoever.

"When they bate Paul in the yard that night, one of them said, 'Now you know who the bosses around here are.' They don't like it to be seen for anybody to get the better of them. They see themselves as the law of the land. Nobody could look at them or say anything.

"People never bothered with them during the Troubles. But when things settled down, they overstepped the mark. They're still trying to be the law."

On the day that his son died, Stephen Quinn had gone to 6.30 Saturday Mass in Crossmaglen so that he could get home in time to watch a rugby match on television. He met another son on his way home, just a couple of hundred yards from the front door of his house.

"Paul got a bating," he was told.

"Where is he?" he replied.

"He is in Monaghan Hospital. His arms and legs are supposed to be broken."

"I went down home and found out it was Drogheda Hospital he was at. We went down. I wasn't really that worried and I thought he would get better," recalled Stephen.

"We got another phone call to say that he had to have some tube put down his throat because he couldn't breathe. We knew the thing wasn't good then. We got to the hospital and were took into a room. They said they were doing all they could."

The medical staff tried everything to save Paul Quinn but his injuries were simply too severe. It was hard to know where to start in listing what had happened to him.

"A doctor and a nurse said that he had died," said Stephen. "They had worked on him for an hour. He was really smashed into bits. They broke every major bone in his body: his hands, his feet, every bit of him. When his girlfriend Emma Murphy got to the yard, she said she could see the bones sticking through his legs.

"That's what they done to him. There was a bit away out of his ear. The side of his head was swelled. To put him in the coffin, they couldn't put his hands across him. He was that badly smashed, they put his arms down by his side. That's the doing they gave him."

In the back of his mind, Stephen Quinn had always feared the IRA would get to his son. He knew they had asked Paul to leave Cullyhanna but even in his darkest dreams he never imagined that they would actually kill him.

"I even knew before it happened that they were after him," he said. "He got warnings about it and to get out of the place. He hadn't a pile of fear in him, he was that sort of boy; he just wouldn't go. He wouldn't be afraid of anybody and maybe it was the wrong way to be.

"I wouldn't ask him to leave. How could you ask your son to leave? I thought maybe one day he would get a thumping and that would be it. Nobody ever thought they would go to that extreme. If they meant to kill him, I don't know. They surely meant for him never to walk again, and if he had survived, he would have been a cabbage."

The community of Cullyhanna in South Armagh has always been regarded as staunchly republican, lying barely two miles from the border with County Monaghan. It is Sinn Féin terrain but, since Paul Quinn died, support for that party has suffered.

"There are people who know things," says Stephen Quinn, "but too afraid to say it. There is intimidation out there but a lot of people who would have supported them support us now. I do believe we will get them. Somewhere along the line, they will make a mistake."

For a family to have a son murdered is bad enough; but to then have his name wrongly blackened afterwards makes it even worse.

"They tried to say it was a feud amongst criminals, about oil. Our Paul here, he hadn't tuppence. They said he was a big smuggler; he had not two pennies," said his father.

"He was living from week to week, getting a bit of work here or there. He would drive anything to get a few bob, trucks, tractors, a digger; he was mad about that. He was no millionaire, far from it. The car he had, an old Carina, is still sitting here – you wouldn't give ten pounds for it."

Joseph Rafferty worked as a courier throughout the week and on Saturday cleaned windows so that he could pay off the mortgage on his apartment. He had bought at the height of the boom in Ongar, a newly built part of the sprawling suburb of Blanchardstown in Dublin 15. The twenty-nine-year-old had moved there from Pearse Street in the south inner city, where he had spent most of his life. He wanted to see more of his six-year-old daughter, who lived nearby, and he planned to collect her from school each day.

In October 2004, Joseph went to a twenty-first birthday party in a hotel in Dublin's city centre. The entire old neighbourhood was there and, after the celebrations, they moved on to a house party.

Joseph Rafferty went home to bed but his younger sister Carmel decided that she would go on with the rest of them. A local thug – with strong links to the IRA – began to taunt her, asking would her brother "Muscles" come to save her. The young gangster said he would sort Joe Rafferty out, then threw a drink at Carmel and kicked her. Another relative stepped in and he was beaten up.

The dispute is believed to have had its origin in a mundane comment made in a pub. The young IRA man had been sitting there drinking with his girlfriend when Joseph Rafferty walked in. The woman made a complimentary comment about Joe, who lifted weights as a hobby. Her boyfriend, already a jealous type, was enraged.

A week after the party, Joseph Rafferty returned to the family home to have Sunday dinner, as he did almost every week. On his way in, he spotted the man who had attacked his sister.

"Why did you do it?" he asked.

"My family's bigger than yours. You don't know what you're dealing with" was the reply.

There were a few "slaps" exchanged.

"The 'Ra [IRA] will put you in a van and bring you up the mountain," were the parting words.

Joseph Rafferty tried to shrug the incident off, make as little of it as possible. His family, however, was already terrified and his sister Esther went to visit a local Sinn Féin councillor, Daithí Doolan. She asked him if he could do anything about it and he said he would look into it.

However, the threats showed no signs of abating. In total, six definitive death threats were recorded, with countless other more minor – but equally worrying – incidents. When Joseph Rafferty walked past any of the gang, they would raise their fingers to their heads as if holding a gun.

On another occasion, they said they would get him at the gym, naming the place where Joe Rafferty liked to work out. It was clear they were already doing their homework on his day-to-day movements.

The family claims that as the New Year began, Daithí Doolan came back and said the problem had been sorted out – a suggestion he vigorously denies. Doolan, who lost his council seat in the last election, said he had at all times encouraged Joe's sister Esther to go to the gardaí and make a complaint about what was happening.

A few months passed and it did seem at last as if perhaps the campaign of intimidation and death threats had ended.

On the morning of 12 April 2005, however, Joseph Rafferty was preparing to make his way to work when he was confronted by a gunman who had been posing as a construction worker. The assassin had stood in wait, a sawn-off shotgun concealed on his body. He was wearing a reflective jacket and a woolly hat and pretended to be carrying out work in the area.

Joseph Rafferty never had a chance – blasted twice, just seconds after leaving his apartment and walking towards his van at around 9.15 a.m. The first shot hit him in the leg, the second in the chest, fatally wounding him.

Witnesses reported a lone gunman who had fled the scene on foot, presumably with a getaway driver waiting nearby. After he was shot, Joe Rafferty tried desperately to run back towards his flat to safety. He fell just yards away on a grass verge, where he died almost immediately.

Gardaí believe the attacker may have been in the area on a number of occasions in the days leading up to the attack, loitering with intent, familiarising himself with the layout of the apartment block and getting a good idea of Joe Rafferty's movements.

Superintendent Gabriel McIntyre, who led the investigation, explained that the gunman would easily have been able to blend in as a construction worker, with so much building going on in the area. "It would have been an ideal disguise for him. He probably would have been here on other mornings. We feel anybody contemplating a shooting like this would have done their homework."

Links to a criminal feud were almost immediately the subject of speculation, with the headline in the normally careful *Irish Times* reading: "Gardaí investigate possible drugs link to murder."

Much was made of a few criminal convictions that Joe Rafferty had for road traffic offences committed in his youth. There were also links to the robbery of a truck but extensive investigations by gardaí showed that Rafferty had not been involved in crime at the time he died.

For his family, though, the motive was immediately apparent. There had been no grand criminal conspiracy or a falling out amongst thieves – it was a simple case of revenge as far as they were concerned. Joe Rafferty had stood up to a young IRA man, and would not be seen to back down in the face of their threats.

Sinn Féin adopted a familiar official stance, grasping at the possibility of a drugs link or a criminal feud, with party president Gerry Adams saying: "Joe Rafferty's killing was a very, very brutal murder – one of a series of such murders in Dublin in the recent past."

Then-Justice Minister Michael McDowell, however, was in little doubt about who was responsible: "A chief suspect in this case remains someone who would be regarded as a member of the IRA."

The Independent Monitoring Commission, which monitors developments in the ceasefire, said that "a member or former member of the IRA" was probably involved in the killing.

The case was anything but clear, certainly not as cut and dried as the murder of Paul Quinn in Cullyhanna. In that instance, the local IRA organisation was almost certainly briefed on what was about to happen.

When Joe Rafferty was murdered, it seems unlikely – gardaí admit – that there was any such authorisation.

In the years since Rafferty was shot, gardaí have made nearly a dozen arrests but are still no closer to catching the killer.

Daithí Doolan, the Sinn Féin representative whose name will forever be linked with the case, has since lost his council seat and says he would still encourage anybody with information to contact gardaí. He said that he had been the victim of an "unprecedented personalised vendetta" led by the media, which consistently dragged his name into a murder and subsequent events in which he had no role. "It is absolutely baseless; no evidence has ever been produced either privately or publicly. It is part of the ongoing campaign against me," he said.

Doolan said he had not lost his seat because of a campaign by Joe's sister Esther Uzell, who had also stood as a candidate in the local elections. "I didn't lose it because of Esther, that wasn't the reason why. The facts speak for themselves: Esther came to my advice clinic on three occasions. I advised her to go to the guards or contact the city council about the anti-social behaviour.

"Joe's name was never even mentioned to me until I heard the terrible news that he had been shot. I circulated two leaflets in the area asking people to come forward. I met with gardaí, gave them every single bit of information I have. They never came back to me a single time asking for anything else.

"I became an easy target and the bogeyman in the media," he said. "I have been scapegoated for something I had absolutely nothing to do with and something I had no control over.

"If I lost either of my brothers, I'd be the very same as Esther. But she needs to be demanding that the gardaí do their job. I stand over my record. I sleep soundly at night. The facts of my case have never been questioned by the gardaí. The media have created this myth, which sells papers.

"The core issue is: why haven't they been brought to justice? What happened to the investigation? The carnival about me doesn't serve anybody: the family or anyone else. Nobody wants them brought to justice more than the family. But second in that queue would be me and when that happens the evidence will be held up, that there was no republican involvement."

For Esther Uzell, the campaign goes on and on. She has been to Washington DC to seek justice for her brother. She has stood in one national and one local election campaign in an attempt to highlight the case.

Her family's message is simple. "Our brother was never involved in any kind of criminal or terrorist activity. He was a hard-working young man. Joseph was murdered as a result of a personal grudge."

4

The Mulhall Sisters: Dismemberment

"Do you believe Farah is dead?" asked the detective garda.

"I can't believe it," said Kathleen Mulhall.

"We are telling you that the body found in the canal is that of Farah Swaleh Noor and that the last time he was seen alive was on O'Connell Street on 20 March 2005 with you and your two daughters, Charlotte and Linda," the investigators said.

Kathleen Mulhall was not much of a liar. Her lover – thirty-eight-year-old Farah Swaleh Noor – had been found chopped up and dumped in the Royal Canal.

The gardaí continued with their questioning.

"Are you saying you don't believe us when we tell you that we have identified the body of Farah Swaleh Noor, that we have established that he was likely killed in your flat at Richmond Cottages?" they said.

"All I could do was wish to God that I could help you, I can't help you," she said.

Farah Swaleh Noor's throat had been slit before his body was dismembered. His penis had been hacked off. He was decapitated; the head has never been found.

"We put it to you that all that we have told you is the truth and you consistently deny it?"

"I done nothing to that man," Kathleen Mulhall said, holding a photo of the dead man, the last remnant of the three years they had spent in an abusive relationship. "That man knows I didn't kill him."

The interrogators pressed her further, saying she had used his bank card after killing him and passed his phone on to somebody else.

"I don't know what you are talking about. The only thing wrong here is Farah is not here," she said.

"You had a hand in his murder?"

She denied it: "All I am saying is that whoever killed him, you are looking down the wrong street."

They quizzed her as to whether she had used his bank cards. "Loads of times," she responded.

"He gave you a bad time?" they asked.

"Very bad," she replied.

"He beat you up?"

"Yeah."

"He raped you?" they asked.

"No," she said. "I'll tell you, Farah was a clean man. He never tried to rape me. Farah never raped me."

The questioning continued: "Did you say Farah beat you up down a lane?"

"Millions of lanes," she responded.

"When was the last time he beat you up?"

"I can't remember."

"Did you need hospital treatment?" they asked.

"Maybe I did need hospital treatment but I didn't go."

The gardaí sensed her guard was down and asked her if she had reason to kill Farah Swaleh Noor.

"I never touched Farah," she said.

"Did your daughters kill him?"

"No, the only one of my family that had a disagreement with Farah was my son John. They had a verbal disagreement. They made it up the next day," she said.

The gardaí told her they knew she had already admitted killing Farah to her sons.

"I told my son nothing," she said. "I would love to help you. If I could help you I would but I am sorry I can't. One day the truth will come out what happened Farah. Then, I want an apology. I would help you one hundred per cent if I could."

The interview concluded. It was 3 August 2005. The truth about what had happened to Farah Swaleh Noor was no mystery; gardaí had already built a concrete picture of what had occurred that day. It was only a matter of time before one of the Mulhalls would slip, before the pressure would force them to confess.

The inevitable breaking point came sixteen days later when Linda Mulhall cracked.

Detective Inspector Christy Mangan had visited her home to talk about "developments" in the case but Linda was not in the humour for talking. He left his number and told her to call if she had a change of heart. It only took a few hours. At 2.34 p.m., Linda Mulhall rang the officer back. She was distraught and she wanted to meet with him. The exact circumstances of how Farah Swaleh Noor had died were about to become clear.

On 20 March 2005, Charlotte Mulhall got a call from her mother asking her to meet her in the city centre. The two sisters – both Linda and Charlotte – travelled into Dublin on a bus where they met their mother outside McDonald's restaurant on O'Connell Street.

Farah Swaleh Noor was there. The couple appeared to be happy, holding hands, but it seemed as if they had already been drinking. They all walked around town before coming to the Dunnes Stores outlet on nearby North Earl Street, where they bought a bottle of vodka. Kathleen Mulhall bought four bottles of Coke, which they mixed with the vodka and drank as they walked. On the Liffey boardwalk, they continued to drink and the three women each took an ecstasy tablet. "They were having fun," said Linda.

After a certain point, alcohol made Farah Swaleh Noor a different man. He and Kathleen began to argue;

they were "narky". They left the boardwalk and walked up the street, arguing as they went.

The two sisters, their mother and the African asylum seeker made their way to Kathleen's flat at Richmond Cottages in Dublin's north inner city. Charlotte turned on the music and sat on Linda's knee while their mother crushed up an ecstasy tablet and put it in Farah's drink.

Swaleh Noor then made a fatal judgement. He put his arm around Linda's neck and whispered in her ear. She couldn't make out exactly what he had said but it was "dirty, dirty". She shivered at the thought of it, knowing deep down that Farah Swaleh Noor was a violent and dangerous man.

Kathleen Mulhall was furious, shouting at him, asking what he meant by saying "We are two creatures of the night."

According to Kathleen's own later statements, she left the room.

The two sisters – who would become known as the Scissor Sisters – remained. Charlotte Mulhall picked up a knife from beside the sink and slashed Farah's throat. He staggered backwards, smashing his head off the bed. Linda Mulhall picked up a hammer and "hit him on the head loads of times, a good few times".

The women were consumed with revenge: vengeance for the pass he had made towards Linda, for the way he had broken up their family, and for the daily abuse he had dished out to their mother.

Farah Swaleh Noor lay on the ground. The devastating attack continued, with Linda smashing him with a hammer and Charlotte stabbing him, until they were absolutely sure that he was dead. The sisters dragged his body into the bathroom where they began to cut him into pieces. They used the hammer to break his bones while each woman used a knife to dismember him. Cutting up the body took a couple of hours, Linda explained to the gardaí.

"The smell, it wouldn't go away. I think about it every night," she said.

They took turns in hammering and slicing up the body and used towels and sheets to try to stem the flow of blood from spreading right around the room.

Linda cut off his penis, and then placed a towel over the dead man's head. She rained down blows upon him, trying to make it easier for them to decapitate him.

When the horrible task was finally complete, they stuffed what remained of Farah into plastic bags, which they then placed inside bigger sports bags. By this stage, Kathleen Mulhall had joined them in the clean-up attempt and the three women walked together to the Royal Canal, where they dumped what was left of him.

The women were already thinking about how they might mask what they had done. Disposing of the body and the head in the same place would probably lead to more immediate identification. Linda Mulhall made the decision to keep his head and Charlotte later buried it in a public park in Tallaght on the other side of

Dublin city, after the three of them carried the cranium in a bag on a bus.

A week after the bizarre burial, Linda Mulhall went to retrieve the head. She dug it up and brought it to another field in her son's schoolbag, where she once again dumped it. Its whereabouts remain the final secret of the case and it has not been found.

On 31 March 2005, the murder investigation began. A man walking in the shadows of Croke Park stadium spotted what appeared to be a body part floating on the surface of the canal. Gardaí were called to the scene and divers waded into the filthy water where they retrieved more bags and more parts of Farah Swaleh Noor's body.

Details emerged only slowly. The remains of the man – at first thought to be white – showed he had been subject to a vicious assault, the victim of dozens of stab wounds. The body had remained unseen for quite a while, gardaí said, and may have been dumped there up to two weeks earlier.

Attempts to cross-reference the body with the names of the disappeared yielded nothing and, as the case grew colder, gardaí feared the torso might never be identified. Detectives even briefly flirted with the idea that the death might have been a ritual killing, a suspicion spurred by the unrelated death of a Nigerian woman the previous year.

As a last-gasp measure, gardaí displayed replicas of the clothing Farah Swaleh Noor had been wearing on the night that he died: white Primark underpants, a pair of socks, and a replica Irish soccer jersey.

The Irish jersey clicked in the mind of Abu Nakaar, an acquaintance of Farah. On the night that his friend had died, he had met him and the Mulhalls on O'Connell Street. Farah Swaleh Noor appeared to be drunk and Nakaar knew there was little point in talking to him when he was in that state. But the replica jersey, he remembered that.

He was reading *Metro Éireann*, the multi-cultural newspaper published in Dublin, when he came across an item about the torso in the canal. The victim had been wearing an Irish soccer shirt. Perhaps it was Farah Swaleh Noor?

Once gardaí were able to identify the body, the investigation began to move rapidly and Kathleen Mulhall and her daughters rapidly entered the frame. Farah Swaleh Noor had been in a relationship with Kathleen, a mother of six from Belclare Gardens in Tallaght, for more than three years. She had left her husband John and moved into a small flat in Richmond Cottages in Ballybough, in the heart of the rough-and-ready part of the north inner city.

Noor had come to Ireland in December 1996 and two weeks later made an application for asylum in Ireland. He claimed he had been born in Mogadishu in Somalia on 2 July 1967 and that he had worked as a fisherman there. He said that he was married and that he had three children. In 1990, when he arrived back home in Mogadishu, he found his wife dead, shot in the chest. He had fled to Kenya, where he spent five years in a refugee camp before paying $1,600 for a flight to Europe.

Most of it was lies; Noor had actually been born Sheilila Seyyid Salim in Kenya. His wife, Husna Mohamed Said, existed all right but she was alive and well and living in Mombasa. Farah Swaleh Noor was an assumed name.

Not long after Kathleen Mulhall and Noor met in Dublin, the couple had briefly moved to Cork. But the move brought no respite from the physical violence which Farah Swaleh Noor carried into every relationship. He beat her on an almost daily basis. In one interview with detectives, Kathleen Mulhall confessed to officers that he had threatened to kill her, chop her up and put her in the fridge. He was then going to eat her, piece by piece. He said he had already killed a young Irish woman in Dun Laoghaire.

This provocation was no defence for murder, however, and the garda net began to close on the three women and John Mulhall, who was Kathleen's husband and father to Linda and Charlotte. On 3 August 2005, they were interviewed for the first time by gardaí.

Within two weeks, Linda Mulhall cracked and gave her confession to Detective Inspector Christy Mangan. The house of cards began to fall and on 14 September gardaí again arrested Kathleen Mulhall. She was by this stage living at an address in County Carlow and gardaí drove her back to Dublin for questioning at Mountjoy Garda station.

The official police interview began at 6.59 p.m.

"You are not obliged to say anything unless you wish to do so, but anything you do say will be taken down in writing and may be given in evidence," they told her.

Kathleen had had enough: it was time to tell them what had really happened.

Charlotte followed suit after being arrested on 19 October. Both she and her sister Linda were charged with murder.

John Mulhall, who gardaí believe may have helped in cleaning up the crime scene, could not live with what had happened. He drove himself to the Phoenix Park where he slung a rope above a thick tree branch and hanged himself.

Soon after, Kathleen Mulhall left the country and moved to England. In her absence, her two daughters were jailed after being found guilty of killing her lover in a trial that transfixed the nation and led to two separate books. Charlotte Mulhall, who had first stabbed Noor, was found guilty of murder and given a mandatory life sentence. Linda Mulhall, who was the first to cooperate with gardaí, was found guilty of manslaughter and handed down a jail term of fifteen years.

Kathleen Mulhall inevitably ended up in prison, pleading guilty to impeding the investigation. She admitted to gardaí that she had helped clean up the crime scene, but it was only to protect her two daughters.

At her trial, evidence was also heard that she had volunteered to take the blame for Farah Swaleh Noor's death. She told gardaí in interviews that she had been in another room when the row broke out between her daughters and the African asylum seeker. She heard "roaring and shouting" as Linda came out of the room, covered in blood and saying that Farah Swaleh Noor was dead.

Kathleen Mulhall went into the room and she saw that Noor was no longer breathing.

"I was dragged out. They slammed the door shut. I did not get back in," she said.

Gardaí asked her why she hadn't reported the killing.

"Why do you think? Because of my children," she said.

Kathleen Mulhall, after living in London for three years under the assumed name of Cathy Ward, had returned voluntarily to Ireland knowing that her past was eventually going to catch up with her. She was given a five-year prison sentence in May 2009.

Farah Swaleh Noor was no angel; of that there was absolutely no doubt. Every relationship in which he was involved in Ireland was abusive. As gardaí delved into his background, a portrait of an ultra-violent man emerged, a man of a furious anger that would be vented on every possible occasion.

He had come to garda attention on a dozen occasions. Whilst living in Cork, a patrol car was called to his flat where he was "very intoxicated and in the middle of the road with his top off". He was cautioned and given a €75 fine.

In 2002, at what gardaí call a DVSA (domestic violence sexual assault), Noor had been observed dropping a knife at the scene but could not be prosecuted.

Two years earlier in Dublin, Noor had twice run into trouble with gardaí after first being abusive to a bus driver and later being accused of assault on an officer.

Not long after arriving in Ireland, the African asylum seeker had spotted a Chinese girl in an amusement arcade in the centre of Dublin. She had special needs and had the mental age of a child. Noor asked her back to his apartment, where "he tried to do something on me. He tried to do something, make sex on me," the woman told the original Mulhall murder trial.

The woman became pregnant after the encounter and gave birth to a baby boy. Ironically, on the night that Farah Swaleh Noor was killed, he and the Mulhalls had by pure chance bumped into the Asian mother and her child.

The following year, he had seduced a sixteen-year-old girl from Tallaght, who was also soon pregnant. She moved in with him not long after their son's birth, but it was not long before regular beatings and rape became a part of their daily life.

In 1999, however, a crime occurred that threw Ireland into a paroxysm of self-questioning – the savagely random murder of a seventeen-year-old as she made her way home one September evening after a night out with friends in south County Dublin. Her name was Raonaid Murray and Farah Swaleh Noor, who was living in the Dun Laoghaire area at the time, emerged at one stage as the prime suspect.

The link was formed following interviews with his former girlfriend from Tallaght, prior to his murder. Her statement says: "I first met Farah in April of 1998 and we had a relationship. This relationship lasted until April 2001. I had one child with Farah as a result of this relationship. I remember when our son . . . was about three months old, Farah became abusive towards me.

"It would have been around the summer of 1999. He used to pull my arm or my hair aggressively. He also forced himself on me sexually a number of times when I wasn't in the mood or even when I was asleep. He was drinking a lot and he became violent towards me regularly, especially when he was drunk."

The woman, who had since married somebody else, recalled how on the evening that Raonaid Murray was killed, Noor had again attempted to rape her.

"I went into the shower to have a shower," she said. "I was undressed in the shower. The next thing Farah came into the shower. I can't remember if Farah was naked or in the process of getting undressed but he tried to force himself on me sexually. I didn't want any of it. The next thing he just snapped. He threw me down into the bath . . . he hit me a few times on the head and body with his fists and slaps."

The then twenty-year-old recalled how she had taken her baby with her and, accompanied by a friend, left the apartment in Dun Laoghaire.

"I remember the next day or so I heard about the murder of Raonaid Murray on the radio or television," she said. "I didn't make any connection at the time."

A few days later, she was back with Farah and he boasted about how he had already been questioned in connection with the murder.

"He seemed to be bragging or boasting about it," she said.

The relationship continued to be abusive.

"He used to threaten that he would burn me and he used to burn himself with cigarettes. He also threatened me with a knife and told me that he'd cut me like a chicken," she said. "He had a Swiss Army knife and a big dagger. I remember he lost the dagger and it was around the time of the Raonaid Murray murder."

Not long after, the woman finally finished her relationship with him. Shortly after that, she was having a drink with her brother and a friend, who happened to have been in school with Raonaid.

"Farah came into the pub after us," she said. "He joined us but we didn't want to stay. He started shouting abuse at [my friend] saying she was the reason why I left him. Then I heard him saying that she was the reason why her friend had got murdered.

"[She] got very upset and ran out of the pub. It was to me and [her] that he was talking about Raonaid Murray because no other friend of [hers] had been killed."

Her friend also gave a statement to gardaí explaining how she witnessed the savage beatings he would routinely dish out.

"He would beat her by slapping her across the head and knocking her to the ground," she said. "She would curl up on the ground to protect herself and he would kick her. He would do this even when she was holding their baby. He had no scruples whatsoever and when he was drunk he would do this in front of anyone, both in public and back in the house."

The woman said her friend had spoken of being raped and remembered seeing photographs that Noor had taken of her "bound up and blindfolded".

"They were of a sexual nature," she said. "She told me that she was not a willing participant in either the photographs or the actions."

She also remembered the night on which Farah Swaleh Noor had claimed he was responsible for the murder of Raonaid Murray.

"He leaned towards me and ranted into my face that it was my fault about the break-up," she said. "I spoke to him and told him that it was nobody's fault only his own. He then sat back down and began mumbling to himself and he was going on about 'your friend, your friend'. At first, I didn't know what he was on about; I thought he meant [a male friend]. He then looked at me and said: 'It's all your fault that your friend is dead; it's all your fault that I killed her.' I was shocked and asked him what he meant. He referred to 'that girl in Dun Laoghaire' because I don't think he knew her name. I was very upset and wanted to find out more but [my friend] just wanted to leave."

Noor's former girlfriend later amended her statement, however, saying she was not certain that the argument took place on the day that Raonaid Murray had died. She also said that Farah could have known in advance of the connection between her friend and the murdered schoolgirl.

A cold-case review of the murder has since ruled out Farah Swaleh Noor and detectives now suspect his threats and admissions were merely bravado. The case on the file remains open.

5

Adrian Bestea: The Body in the Suitcase

History was merely repeating itself when the body of Farah Swaleh Noor was found dumped in the Royal Canal in Dublin. Four years earlier, in 2001, Romanian national Adrian Bestea had met a similarly sorry end, his body stuffed in a suitcase, and then thrown from Binn's Bridge into the grimy canal waters below.

The suitcase had been in the water for around three days when children playing near Croke Park spotted it and pulled it to shore. They opened it to find the bloated decomposing body, wrapped in a duvet and showing obvious signs of head injuries.

Gardaí found themselves in a quandary. When a body was discovered twenty years ago in Dublin, it rarely took even a couple of days before the cadaver would be identified and the family would claim it. However, with the influx of asylum seekers into Ireland that began in the 1990s, there were now thousands of young people around Dublin about whom gardaí knew almost nothing.

Detectives knew he was probably Eastern European but trying to determine from where exactly was always going to prove difficult. Adrian Bestea had not come to their attention for any reason and his fingerprints and DNA produced no matches with their records. Detailed descriptions of the dead man and the clothing he wore were released to the media but to no avail. Eventually, gardaí were forced to take the then unprecedented step of releasing a picture of the man as he lay dead on the coroner's slab.

Finally, he was claimed. Mariana Moraru said the body was that of her only son Adrian. "I still don't believe it is my child. He was my only child and now I have no motivation for life, no motivation to keep living," she said as she prepared to make a poignant journey to Dublin to formally identify the body.

Adrian Bestea, who was just twenty-one when he died, had been living in Ireland since 1999 and had a job in construction. Adrian had left his native Romania along with fifteen other men to find construction work. He had first made his way to Belgium where he bought a forged Czech passport, which he used to make his way to Ireland. Once here, he sought asylum but his initial application was refused and at the time of his death he was awaiting news of his appeal.

Like many asylum seekers, Adrian Bestea had not hesitated in exaggerating his asylum claim, stating that he was gay and was being discriminated against in Romania on the basis of his sexuality.

His mother said: "It is not true that my son was gay. He had been told by the people he left with in 1999 that claiming to be gay was the only chance left to get legal status in Ireland, as the economic reason had been out of the question for some time.

"Romanians talked to each other about this and told each other about these solutions. He had a girlfriend here and lived with the Russian woman for so long. As his mother, I would have known about this," she said.

Adrian was happy in Ireland, his mother said. "He was satisfied there. He phoned home twice a week."

His last call came eight days before the suitcase containing his body was pulled on to the banks of the Royal Canal in July of 2001. "He was happy and had no problems. He told me he was going to get married to his Russian girlfriend," his disconsolate mother explained.

She forgave her son's killers: "I do not hate them. I am not the one who has to judge them. God will judge them. I don't hate Ireland. I have all the trust in the Irish authorities that they will find who killed my child and justice will be done.

"In Timisoara [where Bestea came from] he had everything he wanted – an apartment, a car – but he wanted to fulfil himself, so he travelled to Ireland. All his friends were there. He was very loved in Romania but it was his wish to leave. All his friends had the same idea to emigrate.

"His one wish was to leave Romania and see how it was to be free. I now only have one wish and that is to bring him back. I am grateful to Ireland. Ireland received him and then he tried to fulfil his dream of freedom. I don't hate Ireland or the Irish; I trust them to find his killer."

Gardaí promised that they would find Adrian Bestea's killers but first they had to locate the young Romanian's girlfriend, a Russian woman whom they knew only as Marianna. She had disappeared without trace and detectives involved in the case knew little about her. Marianna had been working in Dublin for possibly two years, was blonde and aged in her mid-twenties. She had come to Ireland to study English. Gardaí had pictures of the couple together and released them in an attempt to locate the young Russian woman.

As the search for her began to intensify, gardaí found her living in an apartment in London. Marina Sourovtzeva – as she was actually called – had fled there after the body was found and was eventually found living in a flat in Kensington in September 2001. She said she would come back to Dublin and cooperated fully with gardaí, providing no fewer than fifteen detailed statements about what had happened.

At her trial, Walter O'Sullivan – who was then a detective sergeant in Dublin's north inner city – would tell the court how the couple had met in a hostel on

Charlemont Street in 1999. They moved into adjoining flats on Strand Road in Sandymount but Bestea became violent and drank heavily.

Marina Sourovtzeva claimed that Adrian Bestea had been violent towards her and she had hired three men from the former USSR to teach him a lesson. They were not supposed to kill him but during the course of a savage beating, he had died.

Gardaí had the witness they needed and on 7 September, just two months after the grim discovery in the canal, twenty-eight-year-old Igor Derjhack was charged with assault. Detective Superintendent Cormac Gordon – one of the force's most experienced detectives until his retirement in 2008 – explained at the hearing how Adrian Bestea had been beaten in an apartment on Strand Road in Sandymount on 8 July. A post-mortem revealed he had died of serious head injuries and the gardaí asked that the suspect be kept in custody as he had already attempted to interfere with witnesses.

Three days later, gardaí brought a second man, Dmytro Semenyuk – also known as Valentins Korelovs – to court, where he was also charged with assault causing harm.

Sourovtzeva claimed to gardaí that she had been the victim of countless beatings at the hands of Bestea but could not report him because she was an asylum seeker and feared deportation.

On 8 July, she was the victim of a particularly vicious beating and fled her house before meeting two female friends in a bar in Dublin's city centre. In desperation, she explained what had happened, and they introduced her to three men who said they would "evict him" from her flat in return for a fee.

She took them to her apartment in Sandymount in Dublin and let them inside, where the men beat Bestea for four and a half hours. First, they spent fifteen minutes beating him on the bed before they put him sitting in an armchair. They hit him repeatedly over the head from 8.15 p.m. that evening until 12.45 a.m.

During the beatings, they took occasional breaks, during which they would drink vodka and wine. They even gave some alcohol to Bestea as the savage torture continued. The men said they wanted to kill him but Marina Sourovtzeva begged them not to, trying to get a taxi for Bestea to take him to a friend's flat. They refused and instead sent her out to buy cigarettes. When she came back, one of the men stood holding a wheel brace in his hand, the weapon that had been used to deliver the fatal blow. The floor, the doors and the walls were all covered in blood.

Sourovtzeva described to gardaí how they crammed the body in the suitcase the following day and took it on the Number 3 bus across the River Liffey to Drumcondra. When they got there, they dumped it in the Royal Canal, hoping it would sink without trace and never be discovered.

By the time thirty-year-old Igor Derjhack came to trial, he was facing charges of murder. The trial of the former bodyguard heard how he and another man, Oleg, had put Adrian Bestea in a chair and tied him up. Oleg was armed with the wheel brace and Derjhack claimed it was Oleg who had "finished him".

An agreement was made that Derjhack would plead guilty to the lesser charges of assault and false imprisonment if the murder charges were dropped. The State agreed and Justice Iarfhlaith O'Neill handed down jail terms of three years and one year to run concurrently for his role in the crime. The judge said Adrian Bestea had been the victim of a "tragic tale of appalling violence". "It is quite clear that you took part in all of these events except the final event that led to his death," the judge said. "This appears to have occurred when you left the flat."

Two months after he began his prison sentence, however, Derjhack was deported to his native Ukraine, having served most of his jail term whilst on remand facing trial.

One of his accomplices, Dmytro Semenyuk, a twenty-six-year-old Ukrainian, also escaped with just three years behind bars. Semenyuk, who knew neither Adrian Bestea nor Marina Sourovtzeva, got a lift to the scene to "teach [him] a lesson", he told gardaí. He said that he had only punched Bestea once before being given Bestea's wallet and bank card and told to buy a bottle of vodka. He tried to take IR£20 from the account but there was nothing in it so he used money given to him by Sourovtzeva.

In his evidence, he said he – and his girlfriend who was also at the scene – stayed there for another half an hour, during which time Bestea was assaulted yet again. When they left, Bestea was still alive, unconscious in the chair.

Marina Sourovtzeva, a mother of one, pleaded guilty to false imprisonment and assault causing harm to Bestea.

She was "hurt, humiliated, embarrassed and upset", explained Detective Sergeant O'Sullivan.

Judge Yvonne Murphy said she accepted that the original plan had never meant to escalate in the way it had.

"The accused felt powerless to stop the situation getting out of control and I am fully satisfied that it was never her intention to have Mr Bestea killed," she said.

"After her visa ran out she aligned herself with some undesirable people who would go out of their way to remain in the country illegally but it was her first offence, she is a young mother and comes from a very loving family.

"Nevertheless the crime of false imprisonment is a very serious one and I feel that the most appropriate sentence would be one of three years, but I will take into account that she will have to serve the sentence outside of her native country and impose a term of two years."

It was almost a year to the day that the suitcase in the canal had been discovered.

The man with the wheel brace had fled Ireland and was never found.

For Adrian Bestea's mother Mariana, the picture painted of her son as an abusive boyfriend given to drinking and violent rage made little sense.

Her only son had loved flowers, she explained in one interview in *The Irish Times*, and every day whilst growing up in Timisoara, he would bring her home a bunch of wild flowers. "Every time he phoned he would become excited as he told me about the flowers he had bought that week," she said. In pictures that he sent home from his new life in Dublin, there were always one and sometimes two bouquets in the background.

"Adrian was a very good child. Affectionate, attentive, friendly. When he was a little boy I always told him I love your little and beautiful eyes. I was sick recently when he phoned, he was worried about me and said, 'Mother, I love your little and beautiful eyes.'"

Bestea's mother said there was simply no way her son could have been violent towards any woman. However, a heartfelt letter sent by her to the trial judge in the Marina Sourovtzeva case arrived too late to be considered.

She wrote: "My name is Mariana Moraru, the mother of Adrian Bestea. In my pursuit of finding out the truth as a mother within the bitter moments that will haunt me for the rest of my life, I wonder how honest can this Marina be with you, for she is the same person that paid three thugs to torture my son.

". . . Marina has also killed the souls of myself as a mother, his father, uncles, aunts, cousins and friends. They loved him so much because Adrian was such a good person, intelligent, of an unquestionable character. He was eager to live a free life and was not a violent man, as this Marina states.

". . . Why didn't she call the authorities when she went out for cigarettes? She preferred to sit back and watch for four straight hours the pain of a man that bought her flowers, gifts, a man that wanted to marry her.

"Could you please ask her, under oath, if my son had indeed hit her with the violence she states? Ask if she has evidence of medical care after the alleged violence, did she get physical marks? Not once when she spoke with me on the phone, did she say Adrian was in any way violent. She always told me everything was OK."

In the letter, Bestea's mother claims that at one stage her son had actually tried to break up with Marina.

She wrote: "As far as I know, my son left her. Marina was calling everywhere crying, wanting to get back with Adrian.

"In her statements, Marina says that she wanted to teach my son a lesson. I don't understand why she had to pay three thugs to do it. . . . I don't want to take my revenge on her, and neither does Adrian's father. We just want to know if what she says is true. I'm convinced that the Irish justice system will set things right, not only for us who suffered so dearly the loss of our only child, but also for Adrian, who was beaten and killed worse than an animal. We hope that these people get what they deserve for their actions . . ."

Bestea's parents found some consolation in the garda investigation; Mariana Moraru described how officers cried beside her as they explained what had happened to her son Adrian.

"In the worst moments of my life, I saw the law men of Ireland crying beside me," she wrote. "I felt their warmth trying to comfort me and ease my pain. On a more personal note, I want to extend a deep thanks to the Irish people, who were there beside me and my son. I will pray to God for their wellbeing.

"We in Romania are left with only the sadness, the tears and a pain-filled grave. We will pray for our child, God bless him. And for the murderers, may God punish them any way he sees fit."

6

Una Lynskey: Death at the Crossroads

Decades have passed since nineteen-year-old Una Lynskey disappeared but the sorry repercussions of her death are still being felt today.

There was a black Ford Zodiac driving around Porterstown Lane that day as Una, a young civil servant, stepped from a bus on her way home from work. The driver of that black Ford Zodiac has never been found; but three men went to jail and another lost his life in the bizarre aftermath of what first started as a routine missing person's report. Una Lynskey vanished on 12 October 1971, her disappearance setting in train a chain of events that would see two of her brothers end up in jail as they administered their own form of justice to a man they believed was involved in her death.

When Una didn't return home for supper, her family was obviously concerned; but it was a time when the

87

public at large were still conditioned to think the best, a time when the random kidnapping and murder of a young woman were almost unthinkable. With each and every day that passed after Una Lynskey failed to return home that Tuesday evening, alarm began to spread like wildfire within the tight-knit County Meath community that she called home.

By Friday, local farmers had been rallied to carry out a massive trawl of their lands, having been told that Una may have suffered a "loss of memory". A tip-off had been received that her body may have been in the River Liffey near Lucan, but a search by sub-aqua divers turned up nothing. Nearer her home, Fire Brigade personnel pumped water from ditches and drains in case she had had an accident and fallen to her death.

Gardaí, however, were beginning to follow what is euphemistically known as a "definite line of inquiry" with information being sought on the black Ford Zodiac or Zephyr car that had been seen lurking around about the time that she had vanished. Screams were heard from the lane and one witness reported seeing a dark vehicle with a young woman struggling in the back of it. Attention, however, began to focus closer to home, on three local men who were seen in the area at the time of her disappearance.

There was a peculiar lack of urgency about the disappearance in the media and the next time the strange case of Una Lynskey merited mention in one national newspaper was when officers drained a pool near her home near Ratoath, County Meath.

In the end, it took almost six weeks from her disappearance to when the body of the young civil servant was finally recovered in the Dublin Mountains near Glencullen in County Dublin.

Gardaí began to piece together a case but as the finger of suspicion was pointed in the direction of the three local men, the anger of Una Lynskey's family was already growing. The wheels of justice move slowly and patience is required of any family while they await the administration of justice.

Una's brothers, John and James, along with their cousin John Gaughan, could not contain themselves. They had sat by and watched as the suspects were questioned in relation to the murder. By all accounts, the men had already confessed, but there was also talk that the men had been beaten whilst in custody.

If ever a violent death in Ireland was motivated by revenge, this was the one.

Abducting Martin Kerrigan, a man from the nearby town of Dunshaughlin, the two Lynskey brothers and John Gaughan took him to the very same spot at which Una Lynskey had been found and dumped him there, battered and bruised.

They had suspected him of the abduction and murder and shortly after Una Lynskey had first disappeared they had already attempted to drag him from a car, desperate to find out what had happened to their sister. Kerrigan had driven into the village of

Ratoath with his sister Eileen. She had left the car to go into a local public house and whilst on her way she met three men, two of Una's brothers and a cousin. They walked past her directly towards the car and attempted to drag Kerrigan from the car. Eileen Kerrigan saw what was happening, returned to the car and tried to pull James Lynskey from the door. She managed to get the door closed as Martin Kerrigan leaped into the driver's seat and tried to get away. James Lynskey climbed on to the bonnet of the car and another man jumped on to the roof. Kerrigan fumbled with the keys in the ignition and eventually got the car started. As he pulled away, the two men hopped from the car.

Eight days later, Martin Kerrigan was collected from his house by a friend and dropped into town at a local pub. He went into Maher's Pub where he stayed drinking from 4.00 in the afternoon until 10.00 that night. At the County Club, a few miles from the town, John and James Lynskey and their cousin John Gaughan were also drinking, leaving the pub at closing time.

Martin Kerrigan was feeling the worse for wear. He had drunk at least eight pints of Guinness and as he hung around the streets of Ratoath, he vomited. Kerrigan was spotted in town by a local garda and given a lift with some friends to a dance in a nearby village called Kilmoone. On the way, the garda came across a car crash and had to leave his car to investigate. He took the two drivers into a house and spoke to them. Meanwhile, the Lynskey brothers and their cousin arrived at the scene.

A row broke out and the two groups of men fought at the crossroads. During the fight, Martin Kerrigan was knocked to the ground and dragged to a waiting car by the two Lynskey brothers.

Meanwhile, the garda, having dealt with the victims of the accident, returned to the scene and summoned reinforcements but it was too late. The car had already left.

In the early hours of the morning, Una's cousin John Gaughan was interviewed by officers after he returned to his home in Ennistown, even before the dead man's body had been found. Gaughan admitted they had "picked up" Kerrigan but said they had dropped him off near Fairyhouse racecourse where he was collected by a grey car.

Gaughan said the row had begun because Martin Kerrigan had insulted Una Lynskey's mother by giving her a two-fingered sign when she had visited her daughter's grave.

Their explanation quickly began to unravel. Further quizzed by gardaí, John Lynskey and John Gaughan admitted they had brought him to the place where Una's body had been found in the Dublin Mountains. Gaughan said there was no way that Kerrigan was dead and that they had not beaten him that badly. When taken from the car, he had lain on the ground, staying quiet.

"I think he was play-acting," said Gaughan.

As the questions continued at the house, the two men asked that James Lynskey be present as well while the interrogation was taking place.

Gardaí noticed that an angry mob was gathering outside the house as word began to spread that Martin Kerrigan had been kidnapped the previous night. The three men – James Lynskey, John Lynskey and John Gaughan – were taken into custody.

A shotgun was found in the back of Gaughan's car while Martin Kerrigan was found dead exactly where they had said he would be; right beside the place where Una Lynskey had been discovered. The three men were then informed that Kerrigan had indeed died.

"Jesus Christ Almighty, we will have to face it," said John Gaughan.

John Lynskey simply replied: "I don't care if I'm strung up in the morning."

His brother James said nothing but was visibly distressed by what he had been told.

The State Pathologist, Dr Maurice Hickey, had examined the victim's body and found a multitude of injuries, many of them minor. Kerrigan's trousers were torn and his shoes were missing. There were cuts and bruises to his face and the skin had been torn from his nose. His scalp had been bruised as if dragged by the hair. The cause of death was suffocation, caused – the pathologist felt – by severe pressure applied to the mouth and neck.

There was also a wound inflicted post-mortem. A three-inch jagged cut had been made to the left side of Kerrigan's scrotum with a sharp implement.

"As a matter of probability, I would think that the wound was produced at least ten to fifteen minutes after the death," said Dr Hickey.

By 10.30 a.m., the three men had been charged and were in custody. Each made statements incriminating themselves, all in disbelief that what had begun as an attempt to find out who had killed Una had ended in another death.

John Lynskey said he had heard that Kerrigan could be found at the crossroads with a group of his friends. When they arrived, they saw him and decided they would bring him away to find out who had killed Una.

He had spotted Kerrigan on the ground and had pulled him by the hair towards the car. As he reached the vehicle, he pushed him inside, but his feet were left sticking out. John Gaughan began driving slowly and as the car moved off, John Lynskey pushed Kerrigan the rest of the way inside and climbed in himself. His brother James then hopped in as the men set off in search of vengeance and answers.

As John Lynskey sat in the back of the car, he had a hold of Kerrigan's head and hand and every so often would shake him, knocking his skull off a bar behind the driver's seat.

As they travelled towards the Dublin Mountains, the men were forced to stop for petrol. Kerrigan saw a chance for escape and began to scream. John Lynskey stuck his fingers in his mouth to silence him.

"Kerrigan remained silent," said John Lynskey. "I do not know whether he was breathing or not. There was no movement from him. I formed the impression he was play-acting. When we reached the place where my sister's body was found, John Gaughan stopped the car and opened the passenger door.

"James and I pushed him out of the car on to the grass margin. He appeared to be unconscious and did not offer any resistance to the fall out. James got out of the car and put his hand on his chest, and said his heart was still beating. He then shoved him into the dyke, which was only about one foot in depth."

Lynskey said the shotgun found in the car had never been used, not even to intimidate the man. They let him know it was in the boot, however, telling him exactly what would happen if he tried to escape. They asked him repeatedly what had happened to Una but Kerrigan insisted that he had not been involved.

"They did it," he said, naming two other men, who would later be charged with the murder.

"He kept saying that," explained John Lynskey, "and settled with that story. He did not go into any detail as to how the incident took place."

James Lynskey in his statement said that he, his brother and his cousin had been drinking in the pub earlier that day. They knew who was responsible for killing their sister, and believed that Kerrigan – and two other men – had abducted her.

"You killed Una," said James Lynskey as they abducted Martin Kerrigan at the crossroads.

"I think my brother Sean [John] said to him: 'You did kill her,' and then Kerrigan said, 'I was in the car with them, but they done it.'"

As they drove towards the Dublin Mountains, the abducted man pleaded to be set free.

"You will stay until you tell us the truth," they replied.

When they arrived at their destination, James Lynskey described how he had lifted the seriously injured man from the car.

"I caught him under the arms; he was very loose. I still thought he was putting it on. I left him on the grass margin just where Una's body was found," explained Lynskey.

"Now that I have heard that Martin Kerrigan is dead, I want to say that I don't know how he could have died. It must be very easy to kill a person."

John Gaughan's story was the very same, telling of how they had dragged him to the car, and driven him across Dublin city; how he was quiet as they dumped him; that he thought he was play-acting.

"When pushed out of the car," said Gaughan, "he sort of rolled in on the bank and remained there. I said to James Lynskey: 'Is he dead?' and James said: 'He is not. His heart is beating. He is up to his old tricks.'"

"The last thing we intended was to kill him," he said in his confession. "We only intended to frighten him. I never thought he was dead. Jesus Christ, is it that easy to kill a man?"

Of the three men's guilt, there was hardly any doubt. The statements made in custody would almost certainly send them to jail. It was – as so often happens – a question of premeditation, as to whether the men should be found guilty of manslaughter or murder. Had they set out with the intention of killing Martin Kerrigan in revenge for the murder of Una Lynskey? Or had they genuinely meant merely to scare him into admitting if he had been involved in her death? When they left him lying in the ditch in the Dublin Mountains, did they realise the damage that had already been done or did they genuinely believe Martin Kerrigan was play-acting and would find his way home, bruised and battered?

As John (Sean) Lynskey appeared in court, giving evidence at his own murder trial, he admitted everything that had happened but stood by his version of events and the claim that they never intended to kill Martin Kerrigan. He admitted that he believed Kerrigan was a suspect in his sister's murder, but denied he had used a knife on him.

The three men were found guilty of the manslaughter – and not guilty of the murder – of Martin Kerrigan. John Lynskey, who was twenty-two, and his cousin John Gaughan, who was four years older, were each given prison sentences of three years. James Lynskey, who was just eighteen at the time, was given a two-year jail term.

By that stage, gardaí had ostensibly found the men they believed were responsible for Una Lynskey's kidnap and murder.

Just six weeks after the Lynskey brothers and John Gaughan were imprisoned, two men – Martin Conmey and Richard Donnelly – went on trial charged with her murder. Martin Kerrigan would almost certainly have also faced prosecution had he lived long enough.

Their trial heard how Una Lynskey was last seen getting off the bus. By 9.00 p.m., her disappearance was brought to the attention of gardaí, with witnesses reporting the suspicious Zephyr car.

One local saw a young woman in the back of a car with a man attempting to kiss her. Shouts and screams were also heard but as regards an actual eyewitness sighting of Una Lynskey, there was nothing.

The case hinged on statements given by Martin Conmey, who had apparently admitted his involvement in her death.

"I want to tell you the truth," he said, "but I can't . . . I can't . . . what will happen to me if I tell you?" he told gardaí.

Hesitating, he broke down under questioning saying that himself, Richard Donnelly and Martin Kerrigan had met Una Lynskey under the bridge. They asked her if she wanted a lift and she got into the car. As they drove down the lane, she began to scream and asked to be let from the car.

"She was trying to get out of the car," he said. "And Kerrigan caught her hand and she fell over with her face against the glass." How exactly she had died was not clear but there was evidence of head injuries.

The late Martin Kerrigan had also made statements incriminating himself, according to gardaí, admitting that they had moved Una Lynskey's body around before finally dumping it in the Dublin Mountains.

After Martin Kerrigan died, Martin Conmey was again questioned by gardaí and this time denied that he had ever hit her.

He said: "I did not hit her. I was in the back seat and she was trying to get out of the car and Kerrigan would not let her out. She tried to get out of the car at the top of her own laneway, but Dick kept driving on. I saw her head go limp and it fell over against the glass."

Another witness said that Una Lynskey had been accidentally knocked over by the men and that was why they had dumped the body.

The evidence of the State Pathologist was inconclusive, however, and no firm cause of death was ever established. Professor Maurice Hickey said there was no evidence of strangulation and no fractures of the bones, which could have suggested that there had been a road accident.

The two men – Martin Conmey and Richard Donnelly – were found guilty of the manslaughter of Una Lynskey and each sentenced to three years in prison.

Critically, the trial judge immediately allowed both men leave to appeal their convictions. Richard Donnelly took advantage and had his conviction overturned.

As the years passed, the scale of garda mishandling in the case became clear as it emerged that Una Lynskey's own parents and a priest had been allowed to question the three suspects whilst in custody.

All three claimed to have been beaten after being detained for forty-five hours at Trim Garda station. Gardaí claim they were never even under arrest and would have been free to leave at any time.

When Martin Kerrigan's father went to visit his son at the station, he found him lying in a corner of the cell dressed only in his underwear.

All he could say was: "Daddy, I did nothing. I did not have anything to do with this."

Whilst in custody, both Martin Kerrigan and Martin Conmey signed statements admitting their involvement. Richard Donnelly would not yield and refused to put his name to any document.

Medical evidence given in court backed up their claims that they had been assaulted whilst in custody. A doctor described how Richard Donnelly had suffered injuries to his arm and a bruise fourteen inches long beneath his left shoulder blade. Both of his ears had been punched red raw, while his jaw was swollen. He had two black eyes and had to be taken for treatment to Navan General Hospital.

While Richard Donnelly was successful in his appeal, for the other man, Martin Conmey, there was no such relief. In his attempts to clear his name, he has taken the State to court, seeking to have his conviction overturned. The case has moved at slower than snail's pace, winding its circuitous way through the legal system for over a decade.

He is still no closer to clearing his name, and the identity of the person who actually killed Una Lynskey seems certain to forever remain a mystery.

7

Seamus Hogan: The Master Burglar

The file sits on a shelf at Crumlin Garda station, gathering only dust. It is one of at least twelve open murder cases in the district, none of which are considered likely to be solved. Detectives based at the two busy sister stations in Crumlin and Sundrive Road are never idle and the younger generation of criminals in the area more than occupies their time. A feud is raging in the area, which has already claimed the lives of at least a dozen men: there have been a dozen arson attacks; gardaí have lost count of the number of gun attacks; and on one occasion a fragmentation grenade was thrown into the living room of a house.

The name of Seamus "Shavo" Hogan is now all but forgotten, a mere footnote in the annals of Dublin's gangland history, and a man almost remembered fondly by gardaí in light of what has come since. His murder

– shot dead by a former IRA man over a petty personal feud – will probably never be solved. There will never be a smoking gun; there are no witnesses waiting to come forward; there is only the criminal code of *omerta*, which will protect the gunman and his accomplices for as long as they live.

Once upon a time, Shavo was one of Ireland's best-known criminals, a member of the gang led by Martin "The General" Cahill, the chief suspect in the country's most famous robbery of all: the infamous art heist at Russborough House.

Now, the only memory of him lies in that little-read garda file. His is not a murder that captured the public imagination. Few apart from his wife Lily and his extended family mourned his death. There are no rewards offered for information about his death and it is not exactly the type of crime that will feature every anniversary on television screens as part of RTÉ's *Crimeline*.

Shavo Hogan was one of the old guard of Irish criminality, a man that gardaí considered one of the "master burglars" in Dublin and Ireland in the 1980s. However, in the years after his former mentor Martin Cahill was gunned down by the IRA, Shavo Hogan had almost certainly drifted into the drugs trade.

It was at a low level, primarily the importation of cannabis, but dark rumours constantly swirled that Shavo was also involved in a gang bringing heroin into Ireland. Hogan had already crossed a number of IRA men and former republicans, not least the man suspected of carrying out his murder, and his links to the illegal drugs trade were ammunition enough for them to carry out the killing under the umbrella of their anti-drugs movement.

The night he died was at least the third attempt on his life. Shavo had always walked a fine line in the dog-eat-dog world of criminality. He was a known garda informer and had once had his ears chopped up to make him resemble a rat. In the weeks before he died, a shipment of cocaine had been intercepted and Shavo Hogan was one of the few who knew about it. Again, suggestions that he was "touting" to gardaí began to circulate.

In the 1980s, Shavo Hogan's mug-shot stood near the top of the heap for gardaí fighting organised crime in Dublin city. By the time of his death, he was simply food for the small fish that swam in the cesspool of Irish gangland.

In the years leading up to Shavo Hogan's death, his name cropped up time and time again in drugs investigations. However, friends and family say that he remained the epitome of an "ordinary decent criminal" until the day he died: a robber, yes; a drug trafficker, not a chance.

Regardless, all those clues and links to organised crime led nowhere and the garda investigation ended up much closer to home. In the Transport Club where Shavo Hogan drank, he had frequently rowed with a former IRA enforcer. The two men had never seen eye to eye and Shavo knew it was only a matter of time before he attempted to take his revenge.

Gardaí have long known who carried out the killing but knowing and proving it are always two very different things. The chief suspect still lives in the Crumlin area, a product of a bygone era, once an enforcer for the Provisional IRA, more latterly a vigilante with a grudge against drug dealers and Shavo Hogan in particular.

The garda file on his death is clinical in detail, all the more chilling for the way it portrays the mundanity of a cold-blooded assassination. "At 9.15 p.m. on the 14 July 2001 Seamus Hogan and his wife Lily Hogan left their home at Balfe Road, Crumlin", it begins, "to go to the Transport Club for a drink." It continues: "They drove straight to the Transport Club, Clogher Road, Dublin 12 and entered the car park. As the car was being parked and Lily was about to get out, Seamus shouted at her: 'Don't get out.'

"There was a male dressed all in black wearing a balaclava standing beside the car and pointing a handgun at the driver's window. One shot was fired through the window. Seamus Hogan put his vehicle into reverse and reversed his vehicle. Two to three more shots were fired at the car.

"Seamus Hogan shouted at Lily to get out. Lily Hogan ended up on the ground. He continued driving in the car park and ended up about 100 yards away from the scene of the original attack . . . where the car came to a rest with Seamus Hogan fatally wounded with gunshots to his body."

By pushing his wife from the car, Shavo almost certainly saved her life, gardaí believe.

Customers from the Transport Club ran from the club shouting: "Someone has been shot." One female witness dialled 999 and within twelve minutes of the shooting two gardaí were at the scene. An ambulance from the Dublin Fire Brigade was already there but emergency personnel could not "render any assistance" to Shavo Hogan, who was already dead. The cause of death, according to State Pathologist Dr John Harbison, was "shock and haemorrhage due to bleeding into his chest cavity principally as a result of a bullet wound to his heart and chest".

A black sports car had been spotted leaving the scene at high speed and was recovered just 500 yards from the shooting, fitted with false number plates. It had been stolen a month earlier on the other side of the River Liffey in Drumcondra.

Gardaí went door to door throughout the area but, while statements were taken as a result of the inquiries, none of the information brought detectives any closer to identifying any suspect.

Fingertip searches of the scene uncovered little. At the Transport Club, gardaí found broken glass and a shirt button, but it appeared as if both had come from Shavo Hogan's own Mitsubishi car. They also found five .45 calibre discharged cartridge cases, two bullet fragments, a bullet jacket, two jacket fragments, bullet core, three .45 calibre bullets, a shotgun wad and pellets that they pulled from the door of the victim's car. Ballistics tests on what was left at the scene found no match.

At Aughavanagh Road, where the getaway vehicle was abandoned, gardaí recovered a pair of blue disposable gloves, apparently dumped by the gunman as he fled. CCTV from the Transport Club was also examined, which shows Shavo Hogan entering the car park with his wife.

"He drives towards the front door and veers right to obtain a parking space," a garda description of the video footage says. "Moments later, he reverses his car and is confronted by two armed and masked men. It shows one of the armed men running first after discharging his firearm [shotgun] to a waiting black Mazda 323 getaway vehicle. The second armed man discharges his firearm and then runs to the same getaway vehicle. Seamus Hogan's vehicle is seen driving towards the soccer pitch."

Nine suspects were nominated in a preliminary list drawn up by gardaí – a who's who of former republican enforcers and gangland criminals. Of the nine listed, five refused to cooperate, two were eliminated on the basis of strong alibis, another claimed to be in a pub, while another man did not even try to account for his own movements but was also ruled out.

"The murder of Seamus Hogan was a professional hit," says the garda review file into the case. "This can be seen by the fact that two gunmen appeared in the car park of the Transport Club that night, one armed with a shotgun and the second armed with a .45 calibre semi-automatic handgun. The shotgun was used to smash the driver's side window and the handgun used to shoot Seamus Hogan a number of times.

"Seamus Hogan was a professional criminal and had throughout his career crossed many people. In the latter years, he focused his criminal activities or drug trafficking. This brought him attention from local Concerned Parents Against Drugs. Of the nine suspects listed over the course of the investigation, the following should be looked at more closely."

Within the year, the garda list of possible culprits had been reduced to just five suspects: four men from Crumlin and another well-known criminal from the north inner city, all of them known to each other and closely aligned with Sinn Féin and the republican movement.

A year before the shooting, two of the men – Suspect A and Suspect B – had been spotted acting suspiciously on a motorbike not far from where Shavo Hogan was enjoying a drink in the Cherry Tree pub in Walkinstown.

"When approached by gardaí, the motorcycle took off at speed leaving [Suspect A] hanging on, he fell off a couple of yards away. After a foot chase, he was arrested. An object was seen to fall from this person as he fell from the motorcycle. A follow-up search of the roadway recovered a fully loaded .38 calibre Taurus Revolver and a pair of gloves," a garda intelligence report says.

"The person arrested was [Suspect A] . . . who declared himself a Republican Activist."

The following morning, Suspect B – a regular attendee at Sinn Féin meetings – was arrested. During a search of his home, gardaí had found written details of Shavo Hogan's vehicles and seized a motorbike. Despite the recovery of the weapon on the day of the attempted shooting, the Director of Public Prosecutions decided that no action could be taken because it was impossible to link the gun directly to the two men on the motorcycle.

While the original attempt on Shavo Hogan's life may well have been derailed, another former republican, a "volatile and dangerous individual", was hatching his own plan to have him killed. This man – Suspect C – had a personal grudge against Shavo, believed to stem from a number of rows in the Transport Club over money and Hogan's involvement in low-level drug trafficking.

"[The suspect] when approached about the Hogan murder refused to account for his movements, stating, 'Am I under arrest?' When told 'No', he said 'I have nothing to say, now go away.'"

On the day of the murder, he was spotted sitting on a wall directly across from the scene of the shooting.

Later that day, he was seen climbing over a wall near where the getaway car was parked.

"[Suspect C] has been suspected of involvement in a number of shootings against drug dealers . . . When arrested he picks a spot on the wall and says nothing."

Gardaí believed that a second man – Suspect D – had also been involved in the shooting, wielding either the shotgun that blasted in Shavo Hogan's window or the handgun that finished him off. He was another well-known enforcer and was also the prime suspect for an attempt on the life of another notorious Dublin criminal, Martin "The Viper" Foley. During that assassination bid, Foley – who has survived four such attacks – was shot in the legs after the gunman's weapon misfired. Foley, a close associate of Shavo Hogan, had dramatically increased his own personal security in the aftermath, explaining in one interview with the *Sunday Business Post* the precautions he had begun to take.

"I had read a lot of books about survival. Well, techniques to avoid being assassinated. I had the door unlocked in the car; I kept it open. It would be a bad mistake for anybody to stay in the car, because if the car is put out of action, you're still stuck in the car," explained the Viper.

Speaking about an earlier attempt on his life, he said: "I jumped over a nearby back wall, into a house and up the stairs. The back door had been open. I could hear crackling. I later learned that one of the guns had jammed.

As I was going up the stairs, I was shot in the back.

"When you are shot on three different occasions and you have eleven holes in your body, psychologically the thing is never going to leave you and you would react to certain situations where anything bad might happen."

The men believed responsible – Suspect C and Suspect D – made no mistake when it came to shooting Shavo Hogan, however; both of them arriving armed, ensuring that even if one of their weapons misfired, they would still find their target.

The fifth suspect – Suspect E – was thought to have carried out intelligence gathering for the other two men. He was a teenage hoodlum who would in later years go on to become involved in armed raids on post offices and banks.

While the media speculated on the cause of Shavo Hogan's death, linking him to some of the then blossoming drug gangs of Crumlin, his wife Lily had other ideas. Her husband had been threatened a number of times in the run-up to his death and she felt she knew with certainty who had killed him.

In a series of interviews with detectives, she documented a succession of rows and threats and a peace-making attempt by Shavo with the men who eventually killed him. An account of those interviews states: "[Lily] states that over the past few months Seamus mentioned to her a number of different encounters he had had with [Suspect B] . . . these encounters generally involved eyeballing. However, one particular encounter which Seamus recounted occurred over the last three months. Seamus Hogan was driving along Clogher Road. At the junction of Clogher Road and Rutland Grove a motorcyclist drove up alongside [him] and made a gun sign with his hand pointing at Seamus Hogan. Hogan stated to Lily that the motorcyclist was [Suspect B].

"Lily also recounted that Seamus has had a couple of 'run-ins' with different members of the Transport Club including [Suspect C] . . . these 'run-ins' involved eyeballing and verbal arguments."

Lily Hogan said her husband had tried to talk to the men, had tried to make peace with them, to bury the hatchet. However, these were not the type of people with whom negotiations would work.

Shavo's wife continued to make her own inquiries locally and in July 2002 named the four men she believed were responsible for the assassination of her husband. None of them has ever been charged and the file on Shavo Hogan's death continues to gather dust.

Shavo Hogan never spoke publicly before his death, but he had over the course of five secret meetings given an account of his life of crime to the reporter Barry O'Kelly.

Those interviews give a perspective on how a man – once considered Ireland's best burglar – became a low-level drug trafficker, for whom time was running out. Hogan spoke about the theft of paintings from the Beit

Collection in Russborough House, the burglary of hundreds of sensitive legal files from the Chief State Solicitor's Office and the theft of guns from garda stores.

During the theft at the Chief State Solicitor's office – "just another job" for Hogan – he had gained access by cutting out a panel in the rear of the premises. He spent three hours inside perusing criminal files.

At John's Road in Dublin, Shavo "walked through the front gate, pretending to be a tradesman" and stole at least twenty official garda firearms during the course of three brazen visits.

Shavo Hogan and the gang led by the General thought they would become millionaires after the robbery of the Beit paintings but they proved impossible to sell. "[I thought I'd] never have to wear a pair of gloves again," he said, "but we didn't get a shilling. Of course, we're bitter."

The robbery had been an exemplar of simplicity. For three or four nights in a row, the men had simply approached the building and deliberately set off the alarms. Security staff at Russborough House assumed there was a fault with the system and on the night of the theft, the alarm was not even turned on.

"Of course everybody was nervous," he said, "but it was easy. The chisel did most of the work. Some of the paintings got damp. It was very difficult to look after them with all the surveillance. Robbing the paintings was the easy bit. Everybody thought they were going to be millionaires. But after that night, everything went downhill. There was a curse on those paintings."

Shavo Hogan admitted that the pressure gardaí put on the gang – portrayed accurately in John Boorman's biopic about Cahill and his accomplices – had eventually paid off. "I don't want to badmouth him," said Shavo. "Martin was like a brother to me in the early days. He was kind, loyal, decent, but the pressure from the police got to him and he changed." Speaking of the garda surveillance operation, he said: "The first week it started, we thought, 'This is great crack.' But it became a nightmare: beeping horns and shining torches into the house at night. It really upset family life."

As the garda operation began to pay dividends, five of the gang ended up in prison, serving sentences for crimes including burglary and armed robbery. Shavo Hogan was one of those caught and it was whilst in high-security Portlaoise Prison that he was attacked and had his ears cut. Released from jail in 1992, he again became friends with Martin Cahill and was a regular visitor to his home in Rathmines. Two years later, the General was dead, shot in his car by a gunman from the Provisional IRA.

Shavo Hogan survived another seven years, sliding into the world of drugs, an area which the General's gang had always vowed to steer clear of. A changing of the guard had come and the real money was now in trafficking cannabis, cocaine and heroin to social drug users and desperate addicts. Hogan was out of his depth and on 14 July 2001 time finally ran out for the "master burglar".

8

Dolores McCrea: The Trail of Guilt

It took six months before the family of Dolores McCrea was even allowed to bury her, the final indignity for them. So little of her was left that gardaí were forced to send samples of her charred remains abroad for DNA analysis. Even that didn't work; the body had been so badly burnt that all trace genetic evidence had been destroyed and gardaí were forced instead to rely on dental records to make their final identification of the remains.

Dolores, a mother of four, had gone missing in January 2004, her disappearance quickly reported to local gardaí by her concerned family. She was supposed to attend a darts tournament in Donegal Town on a Tuesday but never turned up. A major search operation got under way as gardaí almost instantly suspected foul play. Two days later on Thursday, 22 January, Dolores McCrea – or at least what remained of her – was discovered in a field near Ballintra, around six miles from Donegal Town.

By the end of the month, her thirty-nine-year-old husband Gary would appear in court, charged with murdering his estranged wife and then attempting to cremate her remains.

Theirs had been an unhappy marriage, characterised by her decision to convert to Protestantism under duress from him. Friends described how there was always an undertow of violence in their relationship; Dolores was frequently forced to hide bruises under her make-up.

On the day that she died, Dolores McCrea still trusted her husband enough to visit his house. She was there to collect €1,000 in cash for a car that she was selling on to him. It was on this pretext that Gary McCrea had lured her there, offering slightly more than she would have got from any car dealer.

Dolores had left her home in Ballintra to play at the darts competition, driving her red 1997 Peugeot 306, Gary McCrea's murder trial heard. It was about 7.20 p.m. when she left the house, waving goodbye to her ageing father. That was the last time he would see her.

Some time later, she arrived at the house of Gary McCrea. The following morning, her children were already concerned when she hadn't arrived home. It was completely out of character for her not to keep in touch either by phone or by text. One of her daughters sent her a message asking her was if she was okay but it seemed as if the phone had gone dead.

It was not long before Dolores's family and friends began to fear the worst.

Gary McCrea had already made numerous threats towards his estranged wife, even telling her mother that "if he had his way he would . . . kill her". Dolores's mother, Kathleen McGrory, told the Central Criminal Court about phone calls she had received saying her daughter "was not a fit mother".

Another daughter told how her father had frequently alluded to violence. "He told me he was going to kill my mother," she said. "He told me he was going to stab my mother and rip her guts out."

McCrea was convinced his wife was having an affair and was not a fit mother. His daughter, who was fourteen at the time of the killing, had been living with him when Dolores McCrea disappeared. He had been ringing her several times a day.

"He would tell me if I moved in with him, I would have a better life," she said. "He used to go on about other men, that she was a whore. He used to call her names; he used to say she was 'riding' people, that she was a tramp and a walking disease."

The daughter – whose name cannot be given for legal reasons – explained that she had attended a psychologist after the break-up of her parents.

"My father told me that I should get away from there, that I would have a better life. He told me that if I stayed with my mum and sisters, a man [name withheld] would become my new father. He used to tell

117

me that I wasn't wanted there. I heard it so much that I believed him," she said.

Eventually, she had relented and moved in with him in August 2003. For the first few days, it was an improvement but within weeks "every conversation" concerned her mother and it was clear that Gary McCrea was obsessed with his former wife, whom he routinely called "a tramp".

McCrea appeared to be particularly obsessed with a man from County Fermanagh, whom he blamed for the collapse of his marriage. He had already spoken about hiring men to "badly beat" him and warned that he would kill his former wife.

Sharon McCrea, the couple's nineteen-year-old daughter, told how they had moved out of the family home in April 2003. Her mum Dolores had worked in the local pub. In the beginning, her mother had full custody of the three younger children, but Gary McCrea had later won joint access to the kids.

Gary McCrea had offered €20,000 in cash as a settlement for the family home but his ex-wife had refused to accept it. He was furious, believing she deserved nothing from the marriage and that he should be caring for the children. At one stage, McCrea had even asked his eldest daughter Sharon to "speak to the health board" about her mother in an attempt to force full custody.

"He always maintained that mum didn't care about any of the children, that he wanted to get full custody,"

Sharon McCrea explained. "He said that he was going to keep fighting in the courts for full custody, he said he'd fight and that if he didn't get it that he'd kill her. He'd be able to do time for her, that he'd be out in no time and that he'd get his family back."

Sharon last saw her mum alive as she went to play her darts game and by 10.00 the following morning was concerned enough to ring her aunt about what had happened. The aunt, Carmel McGrory, recalled how her terrified niece explained that her mother had never come home. She had by this stage phoned one of the other players on her team, who confirmed that Dolores McCrea had never arrived in Donegal Town as planned.

Carmel McGrory and Sharon McCrea decided they would visit Gary McCrea to ask him if he had seen her. "He said she was probably 'whoring around' with somebody," the court was told. Ms McGrory explained, "I put my hands up and said, 'I don't want to get involved in any family matters but there is her [Dolores's] car.'"

Carmel McGrory asked how she had even made it to the darts match without her car. Gary McCrea responded that she had taken a lift from another person who had followed her up the road. "After we left," Ms McGrory said, "I rang Mammy and said I felt there was something wrong."

At 5.30 p.m. on 21 January, the two women decided to ring gardaí at Ballyshannon station and officially file a missing person's report.

The finger of suspicion quickly landed at Gary McCrea's door. When detectives arrived to interview him, he was calm and collected, stating that Dolores had been there to collect the money for the car. She had dropped it off and had been collected in a silver car by a mystery person.

The following day, gardaí returned with a warrant and began to search around the McCrea farm. Behind some outbuildings, they stumbled upon a large fire, still smouldering. Garda Brendan McMonagle told the court that he had discovered what he felt were most likely human remains in a fire burning in the chassis of an old caravan at the rear of the house. He had first seen a bone around six inches in length with a ball at the end of it. "Shocked and alarmed", he continued his search, uncovering what he thought might have been part of Dolores McCrea's spine. "I thought it was human but I couldn't be sure," he said.

A few minutes later, Garda McMonagle brought Gary McCrea over to the smouldering remains of the fire and asked him why there were bones in it.

"It could be an aul' dog or something," he responded.

Garda McMonagle replied: "I said, 'Gary, you must know what it is.' He replied, 'I don't but I know what you're thinking.'"

"What am I thinking?" asked the garda.

"You think I put her in the f**king fire," answered McCrea.

Another officer, Detective Sergeant Shane Henry, described how he had got down on hands and knees and carefully removed what bones remained from the ashes. The fire "continued to smoulder" and two extinguishers finally had to be used to put it out. Further searches yielded pieces of a Nokia mobile handset and a gold ring, which was "severely corroded".

Detective Sergeant Henry said he found burnt tyres and bushes in the fire and described a strong smell of diesel on arrival at the scene. The fire, he explained, had reached temperatures of anywhere up to 1,000 degrees Celsius.

On the Friday before Dolores McCrea met her violent end, her former husband had collected twenty tyres and had brought them back to his farm, saying he planned to burn some bushes. On the day she disappeared, Gary McCrea had gone to a local filling station and bought two large barrels of diesel, forty-five litres in total. By the time the gardaí arrived thirty-six hours later, there was just one-sixth of it left. A neighbour noticed a "redness" in the sky that day, as if a large fire had been lit.

A local doctor, Marie Drumgoole, was summoned to the scene and she believed that one of the fragments found in the fire was a human shoulder bone.

The fragments discovered in the fire were so badly burnt that the DNA had been destroyed. Pieces of the jaw and teeth were, however, found. Without the possibility of DNA identification, the task fell to the State's forensic dental surgeon, who told the court how he examined "heavily carbonised" teeth recovered from the blaze.

"In my conclusion there is a very high probability that the remains that I examined were the remains of Dolores McCrea," said Dr Paul Keogh. He had compared her dental records with the teeth found by gardaí and found what he said were thirty-five different points that matched. "I can't be 100 per cent conclusive," he explained, "but I found nothing in her remains that I examined that were not in the ante-mortem [dental] record." Dr Keogh told the jury that the chances of two people having such similar dental records were "incredibly low".

Gardaí also searched the house and found yet more incriminating evidence inside. There, they discovered a video taped television programme about a man who had been murdered in Wales. Simon Carter had gone missing in Wales; his body had originally been buried before being dug up and interred again, this time encased in concrete. The killers dug up the body a second time before spending a day burning the body, using diesel as an accelerant.

A second video entitled *Trail of Guilt*, about the murderer and serial rapist Michael Hardacre, was also discovered by the detectives.

The State Pathologist Dr Marie Cassidy told how Gary McCrea had almost been successful and that any possibility of determining the exact cause of death had been lost in the extraordinary heat. She explained that "every cell" and "all the organs had been burned away". DNA analysis had also failed as a result of the "degree of incineration or cremation" of the body.

Dr Cassidy had examined whatever remnants could be dragged from the blaze. She explained that "pieces of skull bone", parts of the lower jaw and loose teeth had all been recovered. The upper part of one thigh, bones from the spinal column and foot-bones could also be identified.

Dr Cassidy said it was unlikely the body had been chopped up in advance of the fire because of the location in which the remains had been found within the smouldering fire. A more detailed examination of the bones took place at the city morgue, but the only conclusion drawn from that was that the remains were those of an adult female who was somewhere between thirty and forty years of age.

Gary McCrea had been meticulous in his attempts to destroy the body but his behaviour in the months leading up to the disappearance left him little chance of proving his innocence.

Even friends described how he had become obsessed with his wife. One friend, Alister McClay, told how he had met Gary McCrea at Christmas.

"He was having a conversation about Dolores and the children," said McClay. "He was very bitter. He never used her name; it was 'bitch' or 'whore'. He made a comment that he was going to sort it out. He more or less said he was going to take matters into his own hands."

McClay told him to "cop himself on" but McCrea already had murder on his mind.

"I'll do time for her," he replied.

On the day that Dolores disappeared, Gary McCrea called to the home of another pal, Eamon Doherty, to say that his wife had visited earlier that evening to sell her car.

Mr McCrea described how his wife had been "a bit on edge" and that a car had pulled up behind her, which she got into. He said that Dolores was "going away for a few days" and asked would he look after the girls.

Four days later, he called Doherty again, asking him to call in. By this stage, the bones had already been found. Gary McCrea had an explanation, however, saying they were "probably lying there for years and that they were only old bones".

On 4 November 2005, Gary McCrea was found guilty of the murder of his wife Dolores by a jury of nine men and three women. It had taken the jury just four hours and thirty-seven minutes to make their unanimous decision.

Mr Justice Michael Hanna told him there was only one sentence that could be handed down in the case of murder, and that was life. Afterwards, Gary and

Dolores McCrea's four young daughters told how they now wanted to move on with their lives. It was left to the eldest daughter Sharon to speak on behalf of her three sisters, who were just children at the time.

"You must remember that there are two families here that are victims, the McCreas and the McGrorys," she said. "My mother was a wonderful mother, daughter, sister and friend to us all. She will never be forgotten.

"I would like to thank the local people of Ballintra, Donegal, who have been there since mummy's death and to the local gardaí who carried out the investigation in a professional manner and who have kept us informed at this difficult time."

Until the very end, Gary McCrea thought that he would walk free from court, believing he had committed the perfect crime.

But his attempts to burn the body had actually made it easier to catch him. In an RTÉ documentary screened three years after his conviction, the State Pathologist Dr Marie Cassidy described how she burnt her fingers sifting through the smouldering fire to find pieces of Dolores McCrea. She explained how fire does not destroy the evidence of the crime and can in fact literally serve to strengthen the evidence.

"[The garda] was very astute and noticed a bone in the fire," she said. "He had the sense to call in a doctor and we were phoned. My aim was to get to Donegal as quickly as possible.

"The problem was the fire was still burning and we weren't sure what damage we would do by trying to put it out. We just had to go for it. And we literally had to do a fingertip search in the burning fire, picking out tiny pieces of bone.

"A lot of people make the mistake of thinking you can destroy a body completely by fire," she explained. "There is a chemical reaction that happens to bone as it is burning that actually makes bones stronger. You cannot totally destroy it by burning."

It was a lesson learnt far too late for Gary McCrea.

9

Julie Brady: The Death Warrant

As Michael Brady wrapped his fingers around his wife Julie's neck, he was signing his own death warrant. He just did not know it at the time.

In a drunken haze, he beat her, raped her and strangled her before leaving her lifeless body in the living room of the family home and going upstairs to sleep.

Michael Brady and Julie had moved into the local authority house in Harelawn Estate in Ronanstown four years earlier. To the outside world, there was no hint whatsoever of what was to come.

Brady, a keen soccer player who worked as a builder's labourer, was, as is so often the case, described as "a quiet man, [and] a great worker" by neighbours and colleagues. As they were quizzed by newspaper reporters, they found it easier to convince themselves that there was a strangler on the loose in the densely residential area west of Dublin city that they called home.

One neighbour described the shock of hearing of Julie's death: "It's hard to believe, it's absolutely shocking. I'd be afraid to open the door. I'd met her just the day before, and she was saying she was getting ready for Christmas, with toys for the kids. When I heard she was dead I thought maybe she'd gone into a coma and died because she was a diabetic."

But Michael Brady was not the perfect husband and, to his wife Julie, he had become anything but the "quiet man". He was in fact a violent man, who would force her into sex and had beaten her on at least two previous occasions. Drinking whiskey turned him particularly fierce and his wife had tried, without success, to warn him about his drinking.

On Saturday, 21 December 1985, Julie Brady – *née* Hyland – was found dead by her four-year-old daughter Elaine. According to reports from the time, Michael Brady was upstairs asleep as his little girl Elaine found her mother lying motionless downstairs at around 9.30 a.m.

It was unusual for Julie Brady not to be up and about making breakfast, doing the things that mothers do and as Elaine went downstairs, she saw her mum lying prone on the floor. She tried to rouse her, but Julie Brady wouldn't move. The four-year-old girl went to her father, who was asleep in the bedroom upstairs, and woke him. He was bleary-eyed but managed to feign surprise and told his daughter that everything was fine. He went downstairs, found his wife as he had left her, pretended to try to wake her, and called an ambulance.

As medical personnel arrived at the scene, gardaí were not far behind. Julie Brady was already dead and detectives immediately classified the case as "highly suspicious". The State Pathologist was called to the scene to carry out the post-mortem; his results saw the investigation quickly upgraded to a murder hunt. The young mother had died of manual strangulation, according to Dr John Harbison, and she was only partially clothed – dressed in a man's jumper – when examined at the scene.

"We now have a full-scale murder inquiry under way," said a garda spokesman.

As officers began to carry out door-to-door inquiries, it quickly became apparent that their perpetrator was, as is so often the case, very close to home. They appealed for anybody who had seen Julie Brady returning home from doing her Christmas shopping that day to come forward to help. Anybody near the house between 11.45 p.m. and 12.30 a.m. that Friday and Saturday was also sought, as gardaí ensured that all possible avenues of inquiry were fully investigated and more importantly ruled out. It is a crucial aspect of potentially domestic murders that other possibilities are excluded so that the defence of an intruder or of a burglary gone wrong is nearly impossible to use when the case eventually comes to court.

Gardaí – as is their wont – were remaining coy the following day as the "hunt" for the strangler continued.

There were no new leads, they said, as behind the scenes the net began to close on Michael Brady.

On Christmas Eve, Julie Brady, a mother of two young children, was buried at Glasnevin Cemetery as her family struggled to comprehend what had befallen them. Amongst the mourners that day was her brother Martin "Marlo" Hyland, a then eighteen-year-old wannabe criminal, who would grow up to become one of the country's most notorious drug traffickers and armed robbers. Revenge might have been on his mind that day but of who had killed his sister, he still was not entirely certain.

Months passed and the investigation faded quietly into the background, at least as far as the general public was concerned. Gardaí continued to beaver away at their caseload, carefully preparing their book of evidence before eventually sending their file to the Director of Public Prosecutions. Early in May, the decision came back – Julie Brady's husband would be charged with her manslaughter.

The twenty-seven-year-old labourer appeared in court accused of unlawfully killing his wife between 10.00 a.m. on 20 December and 10.00 a.m. on 21 December. (Gardaí typically give themselves a wide margin of error in determining the time a crime took place, in case a specific time could be used in evidence against their case at the eventual trial.)

Detective Sergeant Michael Carolan of Ballyfermot Garda station said he had arrested Michael Brady at the family home, the scene of the crime, at 9.58 p.m. the day before. He told Mr Brady he was being charged with the crime, to which the bereaved husband replied: "I don't want to say anything." When he appeared in court the following morning, he was remanded in custody to Mountjoy Prison and refused bail. It was probably just as well.

For more than a year, Michael Brady protested his innocence, claiming he had nothing to do with what had happened to his wife. But as the trial closed in, remorse set in and he decided he would take his punishment. On 3 July 1987, the case finally came to court, where Brady pleaded guilty to manslaughter.

The court heard how the "Gentle Giant" – so nicknamed because of his six-foot-plus height and renowned strength – had returned home from a day's drinking and strangled his wife. Brady was sentenced to ten years in jail. Imposing sentence, Justice Frank Roe, while conceding that Brady was of below-average intelligence and illiterate, said that Julie Brady would have been "in agony" in the last few minutes of her life. As he handed down the jail sentence, the family of the dead woman applauded.

The prosecuting barrister Martin Kennedy said that the young couple had been very much in love and doted on their two daughters, Elaine and Karen.

Michael Brady had worked for a building company but they had finished up at noon that day, because work was ending to allow employees to enjoy the festive period. A party for the employees was organised and free drink and free food were handed out to the group who met at the Belgard Inn in Tallaght. Even before the party had started, before they had even left work, Michael Brady had shared a bottle of whiskey with his work colleagues. He couldn't handle spirits, however, and his wife had even warned him about drinking anything more than beer.

He returned home for a while, long enough to change his clothes, before heading over to the Belgard Inn. He stayed at the party until about 11.00 p.m., according to work colleagues. Nobody knew exactly how much alcohol he had consumed but based on what other people were drinking, his friends reckoned it was somewhere between eight and fourteen pints of Harp. He was certainly drunk, said his workmates, and one of them gave him a lift home as he was in no state to drive. They left him a couple of minutes from the family home in Ronanstown and he walked the remainder of the distance back.

From there, the circumstances of what followed remained unclear as Michael Brady gave gardaí a series of different accounts of what had happened.

It seemed as if Julie had been polishing furniture when he got home. They sat down on a couch together and perhaps they had consensual sex or perhaps he forced himself on her.

Two years earlier, Julie had been diagnosed as a diabetic and her doctor had warned her it would be unwise to have any other children. The couple had agreed to use the "withdrawal method", a then-common (and not very reliable) form of contraception; but on the evening she died, Michael Brady was unwilling to take any such precautions and full sex took place.

Michael Brady had been violent before; on his wife's twenty-first birthday, as she carried their first child Elaine, he had viciously attacked her. It happened again and Julie Brady moved back into her parents' home in Cabra for four months, vowing she would not return unless he curbed his drinking, in particular his appetite for whiskey. He agreed that he would try harder and she – like so many other victims of domestic violence – agreed reluctantly to return to the family home.

A few months before she died, Julie Brady had a strange conversation with her mother. She told her that she planned to grow her nails so that if anybody laid a hand on her, she could fight back and leave a mark on them. Her mother would then be able to determine who was responsible.

From the day Julie died, her mother Nellie never doubted who was responsible. She openly accused Michael Brady of killing her. At the mortuary where the body was held, a row had broken out between the two families, to which gardaí had to be called.

The conversation about her nails proved prophetic and it was exactly this evidence that made the definitive link between Michael Brady and his wife's death.

Under her nails, forensic specialists found his blood, while his face and neck had been severely marked in the aftermath of the attack.

When questioned by gardaí, he said that a concrete block had fallen on him at work and that was the reason for his injuries. The explanation seemed implausible, but there was something disconcerting about the case. Gardaí recalled how Michael Brady gave at least a half-dozen conflicting reports of what had happened. It was confusing, they said, because it wasn't as if he was lying, rather that he hardly knew himself what had happened. The memories of what had happened appeared to have become a dream and Brady could hardly understand his part in those events.

State Pathologist Dr John Harbison told the court that Julie Brady had indeed died of manual strangulation but that she had also been severely beaten around the eyes and face.

When found in the house, Julie Brady was wearing only her husband's jumper. She was face down on a blood-spattered cushion and her clothes had been ripped violently and lay strewn around her. There was blood on her own jumper, which had been stripped off her body. Since it was blood-stained, it meant that some of the blows inflicted on her must have come before she was even undressed. Therefore, the court heard, it was likely she had been attacked before sexual intercourse took place or that she may even have been strangled or partially strangled before he forced himself on her.

In Michael Brady's defence, consultant psychiatrist Dr James Behan said the killer had "subconsciously suppressed" any trauma in his life, including the death of his wife. He had been abandoned by his mother as a child and when he finally got in contact with her, she spent just five minutes in his company before leaving again. Brady did not fully trust women and feared abandonment above all else. The details of his crime were hazy because he himself had managed to block them from his mind.

As Michael Brady was led away to serve his sentence, justice certainly appeared to have been done. A ten-year jail term for manslaughter was well above average and even with standard remission, he would spend at least seven years in jail.

Attempting to prove him guilty of murder would have been difficult because showing premeditation or intent would have been nigh impossible. Besides, that was never the State's contention and nobody involved in the case believed that Michael Brady set off for home that night with the intention of raping and killing his wife.

For Julie Brady's younger brother Marlo Hyland, however, the justice of a court was never going to be enough. The beginnings of a scheme were already forming in his mind.

Michael Brady went to jail and quietly went about serving his sentence. He was the very definition of a model prisoner, according to officers. In February of 1994, he was released from jail, having served his sentence. He was subject to strict conditions and prohibited from making contact with his daughters, visiting their home or visiting their school.

Unlike those convicted of murder, he was to all intents and purposes a free man, however, not under "licence" of the Minister for Justice, rather under the watchful eye of the Probation Service.

Whilst Michael Brady had been languishing in prison, young Marlo Hyland was forging his way into a life of crime. He was not yet exactly amongst the top division of Irish gangland criminals but he was quickly garnering for himself a reputation for violence and the settling of scores with a bullet. By the time Marlo tracked down his real nemesis, the man who had raped and killed his sister Julie, he was already suspected of involvement in two gangland murders.

Michael Brady must have had concerns and he did his level best to live a life under the radar. His stay in prison had been alcohol-free and he had determined to avoid drinking or causing any further trouble.

Eighteen months had elapsed following his release from prison and if anybody had meant to hurt him, surely they would have done so by now? Friends described how they knew of his past but how it seemed so incongruous from such a man. In the pub now, he would sit there, engaging in conversation but politely refusing a pint any time somebody asked.

At around 9.15 p.m. on Thursday, 5 September 1996, Michael Brady's past finally found him again.

Marlo Hyland already knew that he had been released from prison and had after months of searching tracked down an exact address for him. Brady was living in an apartment complex near Ellis Street, just off the quays, in Dublin's city centre. Driving his car home that evening, he pulled up outside a car park. He was last seen putting his hand to his pocket for a swipe card to open the electronic gates that would allow him access.

With chilling echoes of the Veronica Guerin murder, which had happened just a couple of months previously, a motorcycle turned in from Ellis Quay and pulled up beside his car. The window of the car was open and the pillion passenger dismounted the motorcycle and walked towards it. He pulled out a weapon and fired four shots at close range through the gap in the window.

Michael Brady was hit in the neck and upper body and fatally wounded, his seat belt still strapped around him. Death would have been instantaneous, his only consolation that he had not suffered in the way that his wife Julie had.

The assassin got back on the bike as it sped off down Benburb Street before turning right towards the Phoenix Park. Witnesses described the motorcycle to gardaí and some were even able to give a fair account of the licence plate, possibly foreign and almost certainly fake.

The gunman was described as 5'8", of slim build and wearing dark clothes. He wore a helmet and his identity has never been officially confirmed. The description of the driver was even vaguer; simply that he was wearing dark clothes and a dark helmet. Many gardaí believe Marlo Hyland himself was there that day but that, like most other gangland secrets, was taken to the grave.

In the weeks leading up to the murder, the killers had carefully reconnoitred the area, detectives believe, taking details of Michael Brady's movements, the layout of the car park, and the exact location of the flat at a nearby apartment complex where he lived.

On the night he died, he was following his usual routine. He stopped at a petrol station where he bought some groceries for his flat. He drove up to the Ellis Street underground car park, where he always dropped his 1988 Opel Vectra. Had he lived long enough, he would then have made the short walk to the flat he lived in near Arran Quay.

Knowing exactly what had happened and proving just who had done it remained completely separate and the Michael Brady murder file to this day remains unresolved, no significant advances ever made.

Media reports at the time were forced to speak in riddles, suggesting the murder was the result of "personal reasons" or a "grudge". The day after Michael Brady died, *The Irish Times* carried a report, saying: "The gardaí knew that a Dublin criminal held a long-standing grievance against him." Everybody knew Martin Hyland was responsible for the killing, but nobody was in a position to say.

Despite his long career in crime, Marlo never had a single serious conviction and all that the gardaí had on him was a long string of motoring offences. In the world of gangland crime, a string of minor offences like that is almost considered a badge of honour. As one seasoned criminal described it: "It means they know you're up to something but that they can't prove it."

Michael Brady had never been involved in crime, apart from that moment of insanity eleven years before when he killed the woman he loved. In prison, he had made no enemies and the only person who bore him a grudge – and who was capable of delivering upon it – was Marlo Hyland.

For many, there were no tears on the day that Michael Brady's life ended. Julie Brady's mother Nellie for one said she was not sorry about what had happened. Speaking to the *Irish Independent*, she said: "I'm not going behind the door, I'm open, I'm not sorry he's dead. I'll never forget that day. When Justice Roe gave him ten years and I saw him getting into the van, he was dead to me then." She continued: "I thought he'd do the full ten years. I hoped he'd do it. Inside, I'm shaking, but I'm happy."

Nellie Hyland said she had heard two years before that her son-in-law was to be given temporary release on condition he didn't approach his children and that he would be supervised.

"I thought he'd skip," she said. "I don't know what he's been doing. I wouldn't let his name be mentioned in our house.

"I wasn't even allowed to see my daughter after he killed her. He gave her a terrible death. She even had a bone sticking out of her neck.

"The children haven't seen him for five years. They visited him in jail and said they don't want to see him. The little one was first. She went up and told him they were getting on with their lives. They call my husband and I 'Ma' and 'Da' now."

As Elaine Hyland grew up, she was robbed of first her mother and then her father.

On Tuesday, 12 December 2006, Elaine Hyland – by then twenty-six – was returning to her home in Scribblestown Park in Finglas after taking her own daughter to school. As she came to her front door, dark memories of the day she found her mother twenty-one years earlier must have come flooding back.

Her uncle Marlo Hyland had been shot, the victim of an internecine criminal feud, while a young plumber, Anthony Campbell, an innocent in the wrong place at the wrong time, was also dead. Marlo, aged just thirty-nine, had been shot six times in the head after a gunman burst into an upstairs bedroom of the house. Downstairs, twenty-year-old Campbell was murdered simply because he was a potential witness.

Marlo Hyland had been in fear of his life, moving from house to house, hoping to keep clear of the many rivals who plotted to kill him, who suspected that he was weak, who suspected that he had become a garda informer.

A trail of bodies was all that was left in his wake, with the memory of Michael Brady all but forgotten in the bloodshed.

Marlo's life of crime had begun in the years after his sister died; a tragedy that had forever marked him according to gardaí. He began in armed robbery, working with a close-knit group of young criminals from the Cabra area. While some of his associates squandered the money, Marlo branched out, investing it in drugs, bringing shipments of cannabis, cocaine and heroin into Ireland.

In 1994, his involvement in the drugs trade was already well-known and a republican group, which fronted as an anti-drugs movement, marched on a house he occupied in Cabra. Not long after, shots were fired through his front window and he moved his base to Finglas.

Marlo Hyland came of age as an older generation of criminals fell by the wayside, shot dead as time passed and their influence waned. PJ Judge, Joseph Foran and Paschal Boland all died within the space of a few years, leaving a massive void in the drug markets in Dublin's north inner city and suburbs.

Hyland had worked hand in hand with the notorious PJ Judge, a psychopathic criminal with a deserved reputation for violence. Into the vacuum left by Judge and his cronies stepped Hyland and half a dozen other gangs, who scavenged over the remaining territory. Marlo Hyland's influence ebbed and flowed and some local criminals are privately amused by the reputation he had attained by the time he died. "He was not the Mr Big. He was built up by the papers and the guards," said one rival.

The garda were under pressure for results after a spate of unsolved shootings and cash-in-transit raids and Marlo Hyland fitted the bill as a good target. He had a finger in every pie, had built up a substantial property portfolio and had even been involved in a €2 million revenue fraud with former republicans. His was one of the names that jumped to the top of the target-list for the then-nascent Operation Anvil, a garda drive which effectively guaranteed resources and overtime for targeting gangland crime.

Just a few months later, a separate operation – codenamed Oak – was set up specifically to target Marlo Hyland and his gang. The criminal, who was now in his thirties, had become Public Enemy Number One, his blanked-out face a familiar fixture in the pages of the *Sunday World* and other tabloid newspapers.

Operation Oak had immediate successes and in the months that followed, more than €20 million worth of drugs had been seized and thirty of Marlo Hyland's associates had been arrested, with some facing lengthy jail sentences. By the summer, the eagle-eyed officers of the Criminal Assets Bureau were also starting to circle.

In July, firearms were seized at a house that he owned and rumours first began to circulate that Marlo Hyland was now cooperating with gardaí.

Marlo Hyland had also returned to what he knew best. For years, an uneasy peace had existed between rival gangs as they deliberately carved up their territory and ensured everybody was in profit. Their guns, however, remained largely silent as other gang feuds across Dublin grabbed the attention of the gardaí, then the public, and then inevitably the Minister for Justice.

By May, Patrick Harte – a forty-two-year-old drug dealer and former associate – sensed that Hyland's empire was on the wane. He moved in on his "turf", flooding it with drugs and dragging prices down. Marlo had him murdered.

Later that summer, gardaí made another successful raid, seizing nearly half a million euros worth of cocaine and nine firearms in a raid in County Meath. Gardaí arrested a low-level criminal, twenty-six-year-old Paul Reay, at the scene. Fearing he might pass information to gardaí in an attempt to avoid a certain prison sentence of at least ten years, Marlo again ordered his killing.

In November, Hyland made what would prove his final error. A Latvian mother of two, Baiba Saulite, was shot dead on her front doorstep in November 2006 in a brutal murder that appeared to galvanise the nation. That a woman like this could be shot dead in front of her own house whilst chatting to a friend marked yet another "new low" in the annals of Irish crime.

While gardaí had few doubts about the identity of who plotted the killing, what they had not expected was the involvement of the Hyland gang. Intelligence – particularly the use of telephone intercepts – was clearly indicating that Marlo had offered up the assassin and the getaway driver, two dangerous contract killers he had used as enforcers for his gang.

The pressure on Hyland and his associates further intensified and in the white-hot heat of the garda probe that followed, the gang imploded. The garda net closed on the two hitmen while the rumours that Marlo had turned "tout" grew stronger.

On 12 December 2006, those same two assassins shot Marlo Hyland dead. Twenty-one years after his sister Julie died, he too lay dead, shot by the very men he paid to protect him, the circle of vengeance finally squared after more than two decades.

10

Alex Freiberg: A Night from Hell

"It's going to be a night from hell."

Alex Freiberg's mobile phone text message could not have been more terrifying, all the more chilling for its simplicity.

Catherine Shanahan had finally broken up with the thirty-year-old after three-and-a-half long tumultuous years, tired of his constant mood swings, his jealousy and his unpredictability. She had had enough and was determined to start over. Catherine had battled a drug problem but was attempting to put her life back on the straight and narrow.

In June of 2007, as she attended a six-week course to deal with her addictions, she met Kieran Cambridge, a father of five, who was from Cork. There was an instantaneous spark between them and by July Kieran had moved into her home at Carrigeen Close in

Clonmel. A short time later, he had once again moved back to Cork but by September he was back living in Clonmel.

There was a new man around, but Alex Freiberg could not accept it, could not believe his time was gone, that it was truly finished.

A few days before the killing, Catherine Shanahan bumped into Alex Freiberg on the street. They argued and he begged to be taken back. She refused and said she was now living with another man, inadvertently sealing a terrible fate for her new partner.

On 16 September 2007, the text messages had begun, a long series of communications, all written in a fury, as the spurned lover became incandescent with rage.

They came one after another: "Whatever happens it's all your fault."

Next came: "I'm on my way . . . that place is going to turn into a war zone."

Last of all: "It's going to be a night from hell."

In a furious vengeance, he came to her house, armed to the teeth – two large knives, one in either hand – after promising in text messages to turn her home into a "war zone".

Catherine Shanahan was downstairs in the house. Her new boyfriend Kieran Cambridge lay asleep in an upstairs bedroom. Alex Freiberg came inside and held a knife to her throat before calmly walking up the stairs. Cambridge, a forty-five-year-old from Cork, was fast asleep when he was stabbed repeatedly. He was not even given the time to try to defend himself.

Catherine Shanahan rushed upstairs to be by his side as her ex-boyfriend fled the house. Kieran Cambridge was still alive – just barely – and trying to speak, gurgling a few words through the blood that now filled his lungs. He had no chance of survival.

As gardaí arrived at the scene in the early hours of that Sunday morning, Kieran Cambridge was already dead. Catherine Shanahan named Alex Freiberg as the attacker, crying bitterly as she showed detectives the portentous text messages he had sent.

Gardaí arrived at the house where the suspect was hiding, but were forced to wait ten minutes before he would even come outside. Taken to Clonmel Garda station, Freiberg was read the charge of murder by Sergeant Michael Hennebry. He said nothing in reply before being taken to court.

Alex Freiberg appeared before Judge Terence Finn where he was formally charged with killing Kieran Cambridge on Sunday 16 September 2007, some time before 2.30 a.m. that day. Freiberg bowed his head and said nothing as his own solicitor requested a psychiatric assessment, explaining that his client was unemployed and currently in receipt of disability benefit.

It was almost a year before he was eventually tried, what seemed a relatively simple case delayed by the massive backlog that afflicts most murder investigations in Ireland. While Freiberg maintained a low profile during his time on bail awaiting his day of judgement, many other criminals show no such reservations and continue to commit offences. Alex Freiberg instead lay low, as his legal team formulated what they thought could prove a foolproof defence.

Forensic evidence linking their client to the scene was almost non-existent. They would try and prove that Catherine Shanahan was an unreliable witness. The grimly prophetic text messages that Freiberg had sent in the days leading up to the crime seemed the only insurmountable hurdle.

On Monday, 24 November 2008, the trial finally began as Alex Freiberg pleaded not guilty to the murder.

It started badly for him as a local taxi driver gave evidence that he had dropped the accused man in the vicinity of the crime scene on the night in question. Leonard Devine, who said he had known Alex Freiberg since he was young, recalled how he had received a phone call from him seeking a lift that night. He picked him up outside the apartment block where he lived at Bridgewater House in the early hours of the morning. Freiberg said he wanted to go to the Wilderness, the local nickname for a townland that was now home to a number of housing estates on the far side of the town in County Tipperary. Amongst those estates was the Carrigeen, where Catherine Shanahan lived. Leonard Devine engaged in small talk, the standard taxi conversation of those post-midnight hours. Alex Freiberg said he had a couple of bottles of wine with him and was going to visit Catherine. Devine nodded, but he couldn't see any bottles of wine.

Meanwhile, Catherine Shanahan and Kieran Cambridge had been drinking beer with a friend at the house on Carrigeen Close. He had had enough and around 2.00 a.m. he retired to bed while Catherine drove her friend home.

Alex Freiberg was approaching the house as Catherine returned. She was still downstairs while her new partner slept peacefully upstairs. Freiberg entered through the back door and approached her, brandishing the knife. Catherine Shanahan was sure she was about to die as her former boyfriend held the knife close to her throat. He pulled it away and walked out of the room towards the staircase.

Catherine Shanahan did not know what to do; frozen to the spot by what was unfolding, the impending bloodbath, which Alex Freiberg had already promised her.

He slipped up the stairs and into the main bedroom. He plunged the knife into Kieran Cambridge's chest, then pulled it out and plunged it in again. One of the stab wounds pierced the victim's lungs and would prove to be the fatal blow. There were other cuts too, defensive wounds perhaps, but how much Cambridge knew about what had happened was unclear.

Catherine Shanahan lurched upstairs as Freiberg left the house. Blood spilled from the dead man, turning the sheets and duvet crimson. Kieran Cambridge uttered his dying words, but blood already filled his throat and he could not speak properly. Catherine alerted her neighbours and an ambulance was immediately called to the scene. The ambulance went to the wrong house, a mishap in the emergency call and confusion over the precise number of the house. The time delay made little difference, as Kieran Cambridge had already drawn his last breath.

Paramedic Derek Burke said he arrived at the house to find the dead man "lying in the corner of the bed with his head almost propped up on pillows". James Hogan, the other paramedic called to the scene, said the victim did not respond. There was dried and congealed blood on his face and injuries to his right side and right hand, as if the first wound came when he was sleeping on his left-hand side. They moved him to the floor and made a fruitless attempt to resuscitate him; he had already passed away, the hapless victim of a jealous revenge that he hardly knew about.

The text messages Alex Freiberg had sent to Catherine almost seemed to be a pre-written confession, dooming any chance he had of proving his innocence.

His legal team, however, had uncovered another text message; one which they felt could shed a different light on what had happened. Reading from what is known as a "device report" carried out on Kieran Cambridge's phone, it emerged that he had sent messages to a former partner – the mother of two of his children – begging her to take him back. The exact time or date on which the message was sent could not be determined, but their content was simple enough: "All I ever wanted was to live with you and the kids . . . I want my family back."

Catherine Shanahan had, the defence argued, access to this phone and perhaps feared Kieran Cambridge was about to leave her.

Gardaí were also unable to provide a single strand of hair or even a partial fingerprint to back up their contention that Alex Freiberg was the killer.

Despite dozens of different searches near the scene of the crime and the house where Freiberg was eventually arrested, the two knives used in the killing were never found. By the time Alex Freiberg finally gave himself up, he had washed and changed clothes, even his runners. There wasn't a trace of blood on him and no indication of what had happened, no tell-tale wounds inflicted by the stricken man.

Detective Garda Louise O'Loughlin said she had taken a dozen samples from the murder scene but that there was none of "evidential value". She described how Kieran Cambridge's body was lying supine on the floor. There were wounds and blood on his upper body and head. A large amount of blood had dried on the bed and the wall beside while there were blood spatters across the headboard.

Detective Garda O'Loughlin said she had visited the house where Freiberg was arrested the following day. From the washing machine, she took wet clothes, including a tracksuit, a vest, a bath towel and a pair of runners.

As a last resort, gardaí visited Alex Freiberg's home in Clonmel in the hope that they would find something incriminating. A close search again yielded nothing of "evidential value".

There was other evidence that did not appear to sit comfortably with Ms Shanahan's account of what had happened, the defence lawyers argued. A pair of grey tracksuit bottoms had been removed from a washing machine at the crime scene by forensic investigators.

Barrister Frank Quirke said the State was trying to argue that Alex Freiberg had washed away all evidence but had this tracksuit been washed that day? Catherine Shanahan had told gardaí the accused had entered her home wearing tracksuit bottoms as well.

There were other bizarre conflicts in the evidence as the jury was told that Shanahan had actually visited Alex Freiberg in prison on a number of occasions after the killing had taken place.

"Looking for answers," she said, seeking to put some sense on the events that had so fundamentally shaken her life.

Louise Maguire, a friend of both Freiberg and Shanahan, also told the court that when she spoke to Catherine Shanahan about the killing, she was not at all clear about just who had entered the house.

The defence said Catherine was unreliable, accusing her of being a liar. They called her a drug addict and said that she had been trying to buy drugs on the night of the killing. They said she was a "proven liar" and that she had repeatedly "gilded the lily" to paint herself as a good person.

"When you get caught in a house with a dead man you have to think on your feet, you have to come up with an explanation," said defence lawyer David Sutton.

Irrespective of their claims, the jury of seven men and five women found Freiberg guilty of the murder by a majority verdict of ten to two. They spent seven hours in deliberation over the course of two days, reflecting on the evidence they heard. Certainly, there were contradictions in the evidence but who else had sufficient motive to murder Kieran Cambridge that night? How could they disregard those – quite literally – predictive texts? The answer, at least for ten of those jurors, was that Alex Freiberg was responsible for what had happened.

Justice Patrick McCarthy handed down the only sentence he could for the crime of murder – life in prison. At the time of writing, Freiberg has lodged an appeal.

Robert Cambridge, the victim's son, said his father had been his best friend. He was a man who would do anything for his family and for his children. Mr Cambridge said he hardly knew what to tell his brothers and sisters about what had happened to their father.

The mobile phone evidence had proved the ace, modern technology again coming to the rescue of what might otherwise have been a shaky prosecution case.

Emails, text messages, telephone calls and a complex triangulation of mobile phone locations have become a secret weapon in the armoury of gardaí over recent years. In a number of cases, they have been absolutely integral to cases taken by the State against killers and other criminals, which even a decade ago would not have been possible.

The successful prosecution case against Alex Freiberg is just one instance where modern technology has bolstered what otherwise might have been unreliable evidence. In another case, internet searches carried out by a killer helped to prove that a husband had long planned to murder his wife in February 2001. Colin Whelan first strangled his wife Mary, then wrapped her in a duvet to try to disguise the exact time of death.

An analysis of his computer at work showed dozens of internet searches where he had sought out information on strangulation and asphyxiation, and how to try to mask what he was about to do, by claiming she had died in an accidental fall. The internet searches had been deleted but, like most people who use computers, Colin Whelan did not realise that simply pressing the "erase" key does not remove all traces.

Detectives discovered that Whelan had been plotting to kill his wife Mary even before they got married. The investigation into the death uncovered an Irish Life policy showing he would reap a windfall of €500,000 if his wife died within the first decade of marriage.

Whelan was arrested in April 2001 but, after being released from custody pending trial, he faked his own suicide and fled to Spain, where he was working in a bar. An eagle-eyed Irish tourist recognised him from photographs in the newspapers and informed gardaí on return home. Whelan was extradited to Dublin and found guilty of murder before being sentenced to life in prison.

In the now notorious case of Joe O'Reilly, who was also found guilty of the murder of his young wife Rachel in 2004, mobile phone evidence played a pivotal part.

The absence of any DNA or other forensic evidence at the scene might in the past have scuppered any attempt at justice but Joe O'Reilly's decision to carry his mobile phone with him that day effectively put him behind bars.

Mobile phone analysis conducted by Oliver Farrell, an electronic engineer contracted by the phone company O2, showed "a different picture" to the account given by Joe O'Reilly of his movements that day in October. Mr Farrell explained how a mobile phone mast in Murphy's Quarry, close to the O'Reilly family home in the quiet north Dublin village of The Naul, picked up a signal from O'Reilly's phone on two occasions: first at 9.25 a.m. and then at 9.52 a.m. He said it was simply impossible that the telephone mast in north County Dublin could have picked up a mobile phone signal from the Phibsboro bus garage, more than twenty miles away, where Joe O'Reilly claimed to be that day. Nor was it possible for O'Reilly to claim he didn't have his phone with him. Three calls were logged between him and another woman in the hours before the murder took place.

Emails were also recovered by gardaí, which showed a husband very much at odds with the public face he had shown as a man desperately seeking his lost wife. "Me + Rachel + Marriage = over," he wrote in one message to his sister. In others, he referred to her as a "cunt" and ironically as the "world's greatest mum".

"Being a father in this country," he wrote, "no matter how good, will land you with weekend visitations and not much else. Yesterday was my first personal indication of how much I will lose if I don't try different angles."

When Joe O'Reilly eventually murdered his wife, he successfully covered many of his steps. He knew, for instance, that DNA evidence and fingerprints found at the scene would prove nothing. He carefully discarded the murder weapon, the only item that would tie him directly to the murder. It has never been found. After he killed Rachel, he washed himself, ensuring that no trace of what had been done could be found.

Investigating gardaí discovered that Joe O'Reilly had a voracious appetite for watching crime programmes and had picked up hints on how to cleanse a murder scene.

What he did not understand at the time was that the mobile phone in his pocket – even if it was not being used to make a phone call – would prove his undoing.

Like Joe O'Reilly, Alex Freiberg somehow successfully managed to keep his crime scene clean. No trace of him was found near the body of Kieran Cambridge and by the time gardaí caught up with him, his clothes and runners had already been washed clean. Once more, though, the humble mobile phone would prove a killer's downfall.

Like all such technologies, however, their use as a tool in solving cases loses the element of surprise and criminals adapt and evolve quickly. In the 1890s, when fingerprinting first became a popular tool for detective work, the gangsters of the day began to wear gloves to disguise their identity. Then in the late 1980s, as DNA steered police forces into a new era of crime-fighting, wily criminals would wear boiler suits and hairnets to ensure they didn't discard any bodily hair or skin at the scene of a crime.

As mobile phone evidence began to play a key part in the court cases of the new millennium, the world of crime moved on with first drug dealers and pimps, then other criminals quickly discarding mobile phones, thus ensuring they could never be tied to a specific number.

Similarly, few people now plotting a murder would be so foolish as to research the details on a computer in their home or workplace.

And so, the chances of killers like Colin Whelan, Joe O'Reilly or Alex Freiberg being caught so easily may now be a thing of the past.

11

Death of the Innocents

For a single child to die violently is tragedy enough. But for at least sixteen young children to die in such a fashion over the course of just two years seems beyond explanation. It was an epidemic of infanticide and child murder, a statistical aberration that with every passing month became ever more impossible to explain.

To this day, there has never been a convincing account or rationale of what came over Ireland in those two sad years at the turn of the new millennium. If it is possible to have a cluster of suicides, then maybe it is possible to have a cluster of child murders: of parents and relatives killing their own, of young children dying in the most appalling of circumstances.

In the case of Stephen Byrne, the motive for killing his own wife Maeve was simple enough. He believed –

some say wrongly, some say rightly – that she was having an affair. He had forgiven her past indiscretions but when he suspected that she had been unfaithful again, he decided to enact the ultimate revenge.

For Byrne, however, taking the life of his young wife was not enough. As he fled the scene of his first crime with his two boys, ten-year-old Alan and six-year-old Shane, he made a decision that none of them now had any reason to live.

In the early hours of a wet and stormy September morning, he drove his boys to Duncannon, County Wexford. He had been there dozens of times before, spending the day fishing, and his boys would have known how much that place meant to him.

That day, though, their father had other things on his mind. As he arrived at the pier of the picturesque port town, he stepped down upon the accelerator of his white Ford Escort car and it plunged off the sea wall into the cold murky water below. Stephen Byrne could not have spent too long agonising at the scene, for no witnesses ever saw the car leave dry land.

The desperate act was not a spur-of-the-moment decision and Stephen Byrne had made up his mind not long after killing his wife.

Like any case of murder/suicide, there was no criminal trial, no closure for the families, no explanations, only the cold hard facts that emerged at a hearing of the Coroner's Court in County Kilkenny.

The then-Assistant State Pathologist Dr Marie Cassidy told the inquest how both Alan and Shane had high levels of alcohol in their blood, and had almost certainly been fed drink by their dad. The jury of six men and four women listened in a shocked silence as they were told how the boys were still alive as Stephen Byrne drove the car off Duncannon Pier.

The night previously, Stephen had murdered his wife Maeve at the family home in Cuffesgrange, County Kilkenny. She had been beaten before being stabbed three times in the chest and once in the arm in a furious and violent attack.

Stephen's brother Paul Byrne told the coroner Rory Hogan that he had been worried when his brother – who always stayed in touch – didn't phone him. Paul had last spoken to his brother at 8.30 p.m. on the night of the murder. Stephen had said he would call the next day and when he didn't, Paul decided to visit the family home. As he arrived at around 7.30 p.m., it was locked and when he called up later that night, the house again appeared to be completely empty.

"On September 29," he said, "myself, my father Mick and my sister Josephine went up to the house with Sergeant [Mick] Quinlan. Sergeant Quinlan removed the bathroom window as the house was locked up. We were inside for about fifteen to twenty minutes when I noticed a blue towel behind the couch in the kitchen. It was my sister-in-law, Maeve Byrne."

Dr Marie Cassidy told the inquest that the body of the mother of two had been found lying face-up and covered by two blue sheets. She described the scene: "There was a pillowcase covering the head of the body. The body was cold to the touch and naked underneath a white towel robe. The robe and sheets were heavily bloodstained. There were a cluster of stab wounds on the left-hand side of the chest and one which went through the left upper arm."

The pathologist believed Maeve Byrne's body could have been dragged there as there was bruising on her legs and ankles, which was consistent with grab marks.

Estimating a time of death is always an inexact science but it seemed likely that Maeve Byrne had been lying on the floor of her kitchen for around thirty-six hours. The jury was also told that the mother of two had an unusually high level of the anti-depressant medication Prozac in her system when she died.

Dr Cassidy, in her precise clinical language, explained how Maeve had died: "She suffered from cardiac trauma and a severe loss of blood. It is not clear if she put up a defence." The Scottish-born pathologist estimated that Maeve had probably died some time before midnight on 25 September 2000.

What happened in the lead-up to that violent stabbing, nobody will ever know. Was there another argument between the couple? Did Stephen Byrne surprise her, sneak up from behind? Was Maeve able to struggle, did she beg for her life, did she fear for the lives of her two little boys?

Shane and Alan Byrne had been happy at class in the De La Salle National School on the morning of their mother's cruel death. Shane's teacher Catherine Ryan said he was always well-behaved and very bright. "I wasn't aware of any problems he had at home," she said. "He was in good spirits on the morning of Monday, September 25, and he went home as usual but I do not know who collected him."

The last call made from the house came shortly after 10.00 p.m., a forty-six-minute dial-up internet connection, which had been used to find phone numbers for holiday companies. Everything certainly appeared normal and in the week leading up to the tragedy, Stephen Byrne had talked about using a €600 Lotto win to bring his boys to Old Trafford.

After the discovery of Maeve Byrne's body, gardaí set up a nationwide search for the boys, advising officers around the country to watch for the family attempting to leave the country.

Detective Garda Frank McKenna said: "We released a photofit of the boys and their father to the media and set up an incident room in Kilkenny Garda Station."

Gardaí at first just assumed that Stephen Byrne had taken the boys abroad, catching a ferry from Dublin or Rosslare to Britain or to the continent. Then came phone calls describing how the bodies of two young boys had washed up near the village of Duncannon.

Shane, who was only six when he died, was found face down in shallow water at Boyce's Bay by a woman who had been out walking her dog. His older brother Alan was discovered near the scene at the pier.

Detective Garda McKenna continued his evidence: "The keys of Stephen Byrne's car were found in the ignition when the garda team recovered the vehicle."

Dr Marie Cassidy described how the two boys had large amounts of sand and fluid in their mouths and throats. Alan Byrne had an alcohol level of thirty-five milligrams per litre of blood.

"He suffered from bruising at the back of his neck, which could have been from a forceful slap but is more likely to have occurred in the water," said Dr Cassidy.

Shane Byrne had an alcohol level of fifty-five milligrams per litre of blood. It was possible that bacteria had caused the boys to test positive for alcohol, the pathologist said, but it was less likely.

Dr Marie Cassidy explained: "He had no significant injuries. The post-mortem results show he was alive before he went into the water."

Coroner Rory Hogan was left to try and make sense of the tragedy and in his closing words, he could only offer his sympathies to the hundreds of people who had been touched by the awful events of September 2000.

"In respect of these tragedies, everybody is greatly saddened," he said, "which really is an understatement. The losses and gaps these deaths have left in both families is a great tragedy. On behalf of this court and the gardaí I would like to extend my sympathies."

A few weeks after Stephen Byrne drove the family car from Duncannon Pier; his remains were washed up on the coast of Wales. Because of where his body was discovered, his inquest was held in Wales and it was only at that hearing, where local sentiment was not running quite as strongly, that a possible motive for his crime was outlined.

At that inquest, garda divers told how they saw a teddy bear floating in water where the car had gone into the water. Diver Sergeant Tom Lavery told the court: "You get used to suicides and accidents to some extent, but when kids are involved it really sticks in your stomach."

A local officer, Paul Phillips, said he had been in close liaison with the gardaí and said: "The marriage was strained because Mrs Byrne had been having several affairs. It is known she was having an affair at the time of her death."

Philips said Stephen Byrne had last been seen leaving work in Kilkenny at around 5.30 p.m. on 25 September.

Local rumour suggested at the time that Maeve Byrne may have received an amorous text message from a lover, which her husband had intercepted. But in the absence of the definitive answers of a murder trial, that remains merely speculation and the intimate details of their married life went deliberately unremarked upon throughout the inquest in Kilkenny.

What was clear was that Stephen Byrne and Maeve Byrne were still two very different people even after twelve years of marriage. She was extroverted and enjoyed socialising whilst he was happiest talking about motorbikes or fishing and was an infrequent visitor to the local pubs.

The couple had been living in Kilkenny city but it seemed as if an infidelity by Maeve Byrne had forced them on a different track and a new start in the rural village of Cuffesgrange. Despite the move, both were feeling the strain and each had been treated for depression in the year before their lives were ended so suddenly.

That night in September, something enraged Stephen Byrne, be it a text message or some other remark. The couple had already discussed separating and it is of course possible that Maeve Byrne had finally decided to walk away from their relationship.

Nobody will ever know and all that remains of that broken family is a cemetery plot where the father, mother and their two sons lie together.

Fr Martin Delaney, who conducted the funeral service after Stephen Byrne's body was brought back from Wales, said that the dead man represented more than just his "final actions".

"We have seen the dark side of human nature," said the priest. "We will never be able to understand why he did what he did. We can only commend him to the mercy of a loving God.

"Stephen should be remembered for his whole life and not just the last few days. He was a loving father, a mentor, a reliable worker and a loyal friend. When we speak of Stephen Byrne, we should not just remember his final actions. He should also be remembered for the good things he did. He was a man who only wanted to be with his family. Stephen would do his best to get home from work as quickly as he could just to be with his family."

At the inquest, the dead man's brother Paul Byrne must have been inconsolable as he was forced to relive the moments when he found his sister-in-law's body. If his heartbreak then was not enough, the Kilkenny man lost his partner barely fourteen months later, again in the most violent of possible circumstances.

His partner Christine Quinn was stabbed thirty-five times and a blade had been left in the scalp of her badly burnt body. She died of multiple stab wounds to the trunk of the body, to the lungs, liver and heart, including the aorta. One wound made it appear as if she had been stabbed through the nose while the knife had also cut through her hand as she tried to defend herself from a frenzied assault.

As the attacker made his way from the scene, he left a trail of blood and attempted to start three different fires to burn the house down. In evidence, Paul Byrne described how he had spotted the accused man, Mark Costigan, nearby after leaving the house at Greenfields

Road in Kilkenny. Costigan, an eighteen-year-old neighbour who had fallen out with the family, was found guilty of the murder and given a life sentence in prison.

Few families are ever touched by such tragic events once in their lifetime but for it to happen twice makes disproportionate seem an insignificant word. The coincidence that struck the extended Byrne family that year, though, was no more heartbreaking than the grim catalogue of child deaths that seemed to come one after another in 2000 and 2001.

It had begun at a disused quarry on the outskirts of Drogheda, County Louth, six months before Alan and Shane Byrne drowned near the star fort of Duncannon. In March 2000, eighteen-month-old Jack Brennan was found murdered in the bustling commuter town. It appeared as if he had been strangled before a weight was tied around his neck and he was thrown into the flooded quarry.

On February 29, his uncle David had taken him from his bed and pushed him along the Marsh Road towards the scene of the crime where – suffering from paranoid delusions and hallucinations – he strangled his nephew.

Earlier that night, his family had desperately tried to have him taken in for treatment at St Brigid's psychiatric hospital in Ardee, County Louth, but no bed was available for him. Patricia Brennan felt her son was "running out of time", but they had no choice other than to return home.

The murder itself in its initial stages transfixed the nation, who believed crime had truly reached a new low when an infant could be snatched from his bed before being strangled and dumped. The tragic family circumstances of David Brennan and his family's attempts to get him the psychiatric help he needed were not, however, known at the time.

When Brennan first appeared at the district court to be charged, onlookers shouted and booed as he was brought inside. Little did they know that David's family had already forgiven him, realising that he simply was not in control of his mind on that night in February.

At David Brennan's trial, the jury was simply given the option of whether to find him guilty or guilty but insane. To no great surprise, they chose insanity and the twenty-year-old was ordered to be detained at the Central Mental Hospital in Dundrum.

Nobody can draw any specific connection between Jack Brennan's death and the crimes that followed. But it is impossible not to guess that some small glimmer of those stark newspaper headlines about a baby boy strangled and drowned must have come to the mind of those involved in ending the lives of so many children over the next fourteen months.

The year before she died, Catherine Palmer became fully convinced that she was terminally ill and that she had infected her two young daughters, Jennifer (nine), and Louisa (six). Medical tests found nothing wrong and Catherine was subsequently admitted to the psychiatric unit of University College Galway. She was released from hospital after just a week of treatment.

In March 2000, she drove off Tarrea Pier in County Galway, taking her own life and the lives of her two daughters in the process. In her pocket, a garda found a note with the words "This is hell" written down over and again, nine times in total. On the other side of the sheet, it read: "A disgusting waste of two beautiful girls – two human beings."

At the inquest into the deaths of the mother and her children, Tony Jordan, a local painter and decorator, described the scene. Catherine Palmer's Renault car had passed him at high speed before grinding to a halt about ten yards from the water's edge. Catherine had got out, walked to the edge of the pier, looked in, returned to her car and then checked on the two children sitting innocently in the back seat of the vehicle.

Mr Jordan then described their last moments: "The car then revved up and shot forward. It travelled about ten feet before hitting the water. Then it gradually sank."

The emergency services were immediately alerted and diver Eugene Houlihan was at the scene "within minutes". Houlihan dived alone and managed to bring Catherine Palmer and one of her daughters to the surface, still breathing. The second child was pronounced dead at the scene while news came back from University College Hospital that the other two had also succumbed.

In a case taken by Catherine's husband Roy against the Western Health Board for what he believed was their failure to follow up on mental health treatment for his wife, he was awarded €110,000 in damages. All of the money was donated to charities for mental health, women's health and children's care.

Reading a statement after the hearing, the Palmer family said it was unacceptable that such deaths did not lead to a mandatory full inquiry rather than just an inquest.

They said: "We believe that a public understanding of their circumstances would aid other individuals and families in the future. This case was taken for the memory of Catherine, Jennifer and Louisa."

Within the month, another child would be dead, this time killed by her own father after a domestic argument. Leilah Smullen was just three and a half months old when she was violently stabbed six times with a kitchen knife by Derek Hickey.

After he killed the child, Derek Hickey turned on his girlfriend, stabbing her in the neck and back at the flat they shared in Newbridge, County Kildare. He missed her jugular vein by less than a centimetre, a fractional distance that probably saved her life that night.

Hickey later pleaded guilty to the child's murder and was given a mandatory life sentence. He was given a further four years for the attack on Sinead Smullen, both of those jail terms to run concurrently.

In 2009, Hickey became eligible for parole. Leilah's mother Sinead has made public appeals that he not be released from prison, saying: "No amount of years behind bars will ever make him rehabilitated. He has no remorse for what he did. He's not a human being. They should throw away the key because he is a menace to society."

In June 2000, eighteen-month-old Oisin Reilly-Murphy was found dead, having been stabbed eight or nine times in the back of the neck. His father's cousin, John Reilly, a former Army Ranger, lay fast asleep beside his body.

John Reilly, who had also worked as a sanctions inspector in Iraq, had been drinking the previous night with his relative and some friends when a bottle of poteen had been produced.

He drank at least a glass of it before a bed was made up for him in a downstairs room of the house in Tallaght, County Dublin. Oisin Reilly-Murphy was put to sleep beside him and at some time during the night, he met a grisly end. When John Reilly was roused from his sleep, he had no recollection of what had happened.

At his trial, he was found guilty of manslaughter and given a five-year sentence after a jury agreed that he had been the victim of a highly unusual condition called "sane automatism". This effectively meant that a person who otherwise has no psychiatric history could commit an inexplicable act that would leave no trace on the memory. It could come about through a combination of somnambulism and night terrors, an expert medical witness told the proceedings.

During the thirteen-day trial, John Reilly was asked if he now accepted that he was the one who had killed the child.

"Yes," he said.

Justice Paul Carney said that Reilly had been gripped by a "unique, inexplicable and extraordinary effect" and suspended the five-year jail term.

On the morning of 6 July 2000, gardaí found themselves called to yet another harrowing murder scene at Cromcastle Drive in Coolock. This time the victim was just five years old, strangled with a pyjama cord and put back into her own bed. The killer was her own father.

James Byrne had been suffering from an ongoing serious mental illness in the months leading up to his daughter Nicole's death. He had planned his own suicide and his daughter had become difficult to manage, also suffering – it seemed – from a childhood depression.

His wife Sylvia Byrne had been concerned about both of them in the weeks before the tragedy. They had travelled on holiday to Spain but her husband had felt unwell and wanted to come back to Ireland. She had also asked her daughter why she was upset and she had replied: "I don't know, Ma. I love you and I love my Dad and I love James but something is making me sad."

In his mind, James Byrne couldn't leave his wife to cope with two children, their eleven-year-old son James Jnr and little Nicole. Dr Charles Smith of the Central Mental Hospital said that Byrne had been suffering from a severe depression and that it had led him to the brink. He was a "model parent", the trial had heard, but his illness had begun to take control of him.

On the morning that Nicole died, her mother Sylvia went to work at the nearby Cadbury's chocolate factory at around 7.40 a.m. James Byrne dropped his son James Jnr off at the tennis club at around 10 a.m. Nicole had come in the car as well but was still in her pyjamas, having argued about getting dressed that morning.

When they got back home, he took a skipping rope and cable from the shed of his home before strangling his daughter with a pyjama cord. He then put her back in her bed. Byrne then went to the attic of his house where he tried – but failed – to take his own life. He drove first to Howth, then to Blessington, before going to the garda station in Sandymount, where he made a confession.

At his trial, he too was found guilty of the murder but insane and detained for treatment at the Central Mental Hospital. His brave wife Sylvia had stood by him, saying that their family had already suffered enough.

By the time Nicole Byrne died, a clear pattern was beginning to emerge. The cases were not linked per se, but underlying psychiatric conditions had been to blame for, at the very least, the Brennan, Palmer and Nicole Byrne killings and were a possible factor in the case of Oisin Reilly-Murphy. A defence of insanity had not been offered in the Leilah Smullen case, but any man who finds himself stabbing his own child to death cannot be in his right mind.

That July, another young child, Adam Leighio, was the unintended victim of a firebomb attack at his home in Darndale, County Dublin, whilst two months later in September 2000, in a case that is even now scarcely remembered by the public, twelve-year-old Jonathan Kelly was stabbed to death near his home in Wicklow Town by a boy aged just nine.

The sad deaths of Alan Byrne and Shane Byrne in September at Duncannon Pier, it was hoped, would bring to a close a shocking year of senseless and inexplicable violence towards children. However, it was not to be and before the year was out the families of two more young children would be forced to watch as a white coffin was lowered into a grave after horrific family tragedies.

On 28 October 2000, Jacqueline Costello grabbed her eight-year-old son Robert by the throat and strangled him. In a statement, Costello – who was almost certainly an undiagnosed schizophrenic – described how she didn't even know she had the strength to do it.

"They [her children] were running around me. I had no rest at all. I just wanted to clean up and be normal," she said. "I don't know what happened. [I said to Robert] you know what has to be done, take some sleeping tablets. He said: 'I don't want them, I want to live, I want to live.'

"'You'll be grand, you'll be doing us all a favour,'" she replied.

"I don't know where I got the strength. I put my hand around his throat. I just made sure he died. I couldn't look, I felt so sick. I just couldn't believe what happened to me."

Detectives and other officers involved in the case had little interest in seeing Costello go to prison for the events which took place that day at the family home in Mullinavat, County Kilkenny. Once again, it was patently clear that gardaí were dealing with a vulnerable person who was not in control when they committed the terrible act.

Dr Brian McCaffrey, a forensic psychiatrist, said he believed that Jacqueline Costello had been "a misdiagnosed schizophrenic" and that if she had been listened to, Robert's death could well have been avoided. On the day of his death, Jacqueline Costello had also visited a psychiatric hospital but she was not admitted.

It took the jury less than twenty minutes to find her guilty of murder but insane. This was the only option open to them as at the time the more recently introduced option of finding a person not guilty by reason of insanity was not available.

For the family of nine-year-old Miriam Burke, there would be no murder trial as her father Michael chose to take his own life as well. On 7 December, the unemployed fisherman – who had been suffering from severe depression – drove himself and his little daughter off the pier at Howth in north County Dublin. Michael Burke had been worried about having no work with Christmas approaching, as he drove his daughter to school that morning.

His partner Lillian McGowan gave a statement, which was read out at Dublin's Coroner's Court, in which she said she had been somewhat concerned when she noticed her blue Fiesta car absent from her driveway.

Gardaí asked her whether the couple had been close in the months leading up to the tragedy. "We talked all the time and told each other we loved each other very much," she said. Their relationship had not been in difficulty.

Diver Lorcan Dignam recalled how he found the car about four metres under the surface of the water off the East Pier of Howth Harbour. It was difficult to see anything but Burke's body appeared to be jammed in the driver's window of the vehicle, the instinctive actions of the drowning man.

The fifty-one-year-old was rushed to hospital but attempts to resuscitate him failed and he was pronounced dead just fifty minutes before the body of Miriam, dressed in her school uniform, was taken from the car at 3.30 p.m.

As the New Year began, the grim catalogue of death showed some signs of relenting but it wasn't long before the murders began again.

Somalian Yusif Ali Abdi had been severely mentally ill in the months leading up to his son's death. He had been arrested by gardaí after stepping out in front of a patrol van and firmly believed the Irish police were out to get him, tapping his phones and installing CCTV cameras to film him.

In April 2001, he took his young child Nathan from his cot at an apartment in Clane, County Kildare, and banged the child's head off a wall three times. Two years later, Yusif Ali Abdi was found guilty of the murder of his twenty-month-old son despite overwhelming evidence that he was a schizophrenic suffering from severe delusions.

He was also suffering from post-traumatic stress, having seen his parents shot dead and spending five years in a refugee camp in Africa. As he was being led away, he shouted: "This is racism, this is racism."

Two months after little Nathan Baraka Andrew Ali died, the body of eight-year-old Karl Murphy was found in shallow water on the seashore at Greystones, County Wicklow. His mother Ruth was found sitting in a nearby cave, in an "incoherent" state, her clothes wet.

Ruth Murphy had had supervised access to her child following the break-up of her marriage some two years previously. She had developed a chronic drink problem and had been the subject of a barring order prohibiting her from going anywhere near the family home in Ashford, County Wicklow.

On the morning of Karl's death, he was being minded in a friend's house when Ruth Murphy arrived to see him. When the child minders were not watching, she had taken her son and driven him directly to the beach, where she had drowned him.

A post-mortem had found bruising on his back and shoulders and tell-tale "finger-sized" bruises on the back of his neck, which suggested "forcible drowning". His mother was drunk at the time and traces of the psychiatric drug Librium were found in her system. Ruth Murphy, who was forty-two at the time of trial, pleaded guilty to murder and was given a mandatory life sentence.

Worse was to follow Karl Murphy's death when news began to emerge in July 2001 of another tragedy, this time involving the deaths of a mother and her two sons, who were aged nine and seven. Again, gardaí were in no doubt as to who was responsible and this time the perpetrator had stayed alive to face repercussions.

Gregory Fox, originally from Dublin but living in Castledaly, County Westmeath, admitted killing his wife Debbie because she was having an affair. After murdering her, he took a knife to his two sons Trevor and Killian because he did not want them to live to see their mother dead.

Fox had pleaded with Debbie not to leave him before a massive row began. He smashed a beer bottle in her throat, and then stabbed her repeatedly before using a hurley to beat her over the head. He stabbed his two children with a butcher's knife even after they awoke and tried to defend themselves.

The court heard how he had committed acts of which he never had thought himself capable before he was given three separate life sentences and taken to prison.

Those two sad years at the turn of the new century left parents right across the country perplexed. Traditional wisdom had it that a child was safest when indoors, when collected from school, when in a friend's house or when avoiding lifts from strangers. Yet the reality was turning out to be something quite different. The chances of a youngster being killed by a random stranger in Ireland are almost non-existent; the chances of them dying at the hands of someone they know much higher. Danger did not begin on the unsupervised streets. Rather, the real danger lay at home.

12.

Jacqui and Kelly Noble:
Like Mother, Like Daughter

He used to tie her to a chair or bed and anally rape her.
He would kick and beat her, with his fists or with
weapons. As Jacqui Noble recounted the unspeakable
depravity inflicted upon her by the late Derek Benson,
she turned her face from the court in shame, unable to
face anybody in the room.

Ms Noble was fighting for her freedom and
detectives would – in most instances – have believed she
was exaggerating. A slight exaggeration or a small fib
can be enough to sway a jury, sow the seeds of doubt
and sympathy in their minds. But for the gardaí that sat
watching Ms Noble, they knew there were no lies.
There was no need of exaggeration.

Like many brutal men, Derek Benson would meet a
brutal end: stabbed with a sword more than twenty-

five times until he was dead, his head almost cut loose from his body.

Jacqui Noble had endured more suffering than anybody could possibly deserve. And, like most victims of domestic violence, she found it impossible to run away. She had planned, plotted and formulated her escape over and over again but she knew that Derek Benson would come after her. He had promised to find her – and when it came to threats of violence, he was a man who delivered on his promises.

Noble, who was thirty-eight when she went on trial for his murder, had met Benson when she was just sixteen. In common with many abusive men, he tried at first to wear a veil of normality, but the mask slipped after just six months. "He gave me a kick into the face at Halloween, he busted my eye," Jacqui Noble told her murder trial.

From there, the downward spiral began: years of physical and sexual abuse, forced anal and oral sex, beatings with fists and feet, even attacks on her family.

Jacqui Noble became pregnant and, after talking to her mother, decided to have an abortion. Her parents were already deeply concerned about the relationship and begged her to keep clear of Derek Benson, knowing he was trouble.

Noble again became pregnant and this time had a baby girl, whom the couple named Kelly. The birth of the child did nothing to curb Benson's behaviour.

At the christening, Benson was drinking, yet again. He smashed in the windows of her parents' house and bit her father on the back. "To the day he died he had two bite marks on his back," Jacqui Noble recalled.

On another occasion, he split open one of her eyes because the dinner she had made was "not right on the plate". He used to deliberately beat her on the back so that nobody else would see the bruises. Asked about the nature of the abuse, she replied: "Fists, feet, whatever he could get his hands on."

Her neighbour, Claire Keely, told how she had seen Jacqui beaten with a plank at one stage because she hadn't prepared breakfast for Benson.

On another occasion, he chased her from the house, as Claire Keely explained: "He ran out after her into my bedroom . . . he was killing her." When he did finally catch up with her, he beat and kicked her on the ground.

The first time that she met Ms Noble, Claire noticed that her hand was badly swollen. "She [Jacqui] said she did not get up to make Derek's breakfast that morning and he hit her with a plank," said Keeley.

Benson was violent towards the couple's young daughter and spared no mercy towards her despite her tender years. Gardaí were called on one occasion, suspecting an assault on his daughter, but Benson was back at the family's flat in Dublin's Ballymun the next morning.

Jacqui Noble told how she would literally wake to a nightmare in the morning to find him looming over her. "[Often], he would be right over me with a balaclava and a knife up to my throat," she said. "I just had enough; my brain was exploding with everything."

Her doctor, Muiris Houston, gave evidence that backed up every claim she made. He had treated her in April 1994, again in 1996, in 1997, in 1998 and again in February 1999, before he left the practice. Ms Noble had suffered a catalogue of injuries including fractured ribs, bruises to the chest and breasts, kicks to the back and shoulder with extensive bruising to the body and thighs. On at least two occasions, she had to be referred to a casualty ward for x-rays.

Dr Houston said her sole concern was her child Kelly: "Jacqui was an excellent mother, someone who cared for her daughter extremely well." Dr Houston advised her to contact the gardaí but the cycle of abuse continued.

Not content with ruining Jacqui Noble's life, Derek Benson was also turning his own daughter Kelly into a drug addict, allowing her to drink and smoke hash; he even taught her how to inject heroin.

Jacqui Noble got a barring order against him but he repeatedly broke it and at one stage assaulted a female garda who came to enforce it. "[I] just wanted to get away from him. To let me and Kelly live in peace," she said.

After giving birth to Kelly, Jacqui Noble had gone through a further three abortions, determined that she would not have another child born in that environment. She left home time and time again, desperately seeking refuge with her friends and family. "I was like a bag lady, always going to stay somewhere else," she said.

Asked why she had not left permanently, she said: "He always told me if I left he'd find me anywhere and he'd cut Kelly up in front of me and he'd cut me up." Jacqui Noble had no reason to doubt him. All her options exhausted, she decided that her only choice was to do away with him once and for all.

After more than twenty years of abuse, she set her sights on vengeance and deliverance from his evil. Ms Noble approached her friend, twenty-four-year-old pub doorman Paul Hopkins, and asked him if he would help. The State would claim there was a financial motive but, irrespective of that, Benson's fate was sealed.

On 13 May 2000, Derek Benson's remains – stabbed more than two dozen times and run through with a sword – were found at the couple's flat at Sandy Hill Avenue. It appeared as if an attempt had been made to decapitate him.

The then Deputy State Pathologist Dr Marie Cassidy revealed to the joint murder trial of Ms Noble and Mr Hopkins that Derek Benson had been stabbed twenty-five times and that some of the wounds had pierced "from back to front and front to back". He had suffered another sixty cutting wounds which extended the length of his body, from the top of his head to his feet.

The Central Criminal Court heard that one of the wounds was "gaping" and had cut through the spine around the neck. It was a "slicing or hacking injury", as if the killer had tried to chop his head off. There were wounds to his arms and hands and the tendons of his muscles had been severed as if Benson had tried to protect himself from the onslaught.

Dr Cassidy said it was a "sustained and vicious assault" and that the dead man was lying on the ground when some of the wounds were inflicted. The cause of death was simple, she said: "Multiple stab, incise and cutting injuries to the head, trunk and limbs."

On the night of the killing, their neighbour Claire Keely described how she heard the grim screams of death emanating from the flat at about 3.00 a.m. She could hear Derek Benson yelling for mercy, crying: "For God's sake . . . for f**k's sake." Smoke and fire began billowing from the flat as she called the emergency services.

The arrangement between Noble and Hopkins had come to fruition and now the garda investigation would begin.

There were precious few doubts about the abuse handed out to Jacqui Noble over the course of more than two decades. However, a new potential motive was also emerging, one which had less to do with domestic violence and one which pointed in the direction of a financial imperative.

Jacqui Noble was due a tidy inheritance after the deaths of her parents and Derek Benson already had his mind made up about how it was to be spent. He wanted money for an apartment and a motorbike and Jacqui Noble knew that what Derek wanted, Derek usually got.

Detectives believed that Noble and Hopkins had agreed a price of between IR£3,000 and IR£5,000 for a contract killing. Just IR£200 had been paid up front, with the rest to be handed over on completion.

Tom O'Connell, the senior counsel acting for the State, outlined a financial motive as old as mankind: "The plan was that Mr Hopkins would actually kill Mr Benson and that he would do this at the request of Ms Noble who paid him a certain amount of money up front and agreed to pay him more after he was killed."

However, even those prosecuting Jacqui Noble admitted that thoughts of killing her partner had been around "for some time", far longer than the inheritance.

On 11 May 2000, just two days before the killing, Jacqui Noble met with Paul Hopkins to finalise their deal and handed over IR£200. Hopkins bought a sword from his brother, some sleeping tablets and a mobile phone. He handed over the phone and tablets to Noble.

Senior Counsel Tom O'Connell continued: "It was agreed that she would go to the flat and drug Mr Benson and that she would then contact Mr Hopkins by phone when the coast was clear. She would then leave and he would kill him."

Derek Benson's violence was not limited to Jacqui Noble; Paul Hopkins had also suffered his rage. He told the court how he had been bullied, threatened and assaulted by Benson, who had also threatened his girlfriend and their baby daughter that he would burn them after he "was finished with [raping] them".

Jacqui Noble and Paul Hopkins were jailed for life in February 2004 after a jury of seven men and five women returned a unanimous verdict. Two of the female jurors were in tears as the verdict was read out. Jacqui Noble cried while relatives, friends and family of both her and Paul Hopkins sobbed at the back of the court.

Kelly Noble was not in court on the day her mother was convicted, having already been taken into foster care. She remained close to her mother, however, visiting her every Saturday in the Dóchas Women's Prison at the Mountjoy complex in Dublin's north inner city.

In a famous interview with presenter Joe Duffy on RTÉ's *Liveline*, she gave her mother her full support. "My father that she killed was an animal," she said, her voice quivering. "He didn't treat either of us with respect and he was basically an animal. He made our lives hell.

"My Ma put up with life with my Da and now she is serving a life sentence in Mountjoy Women's Prison."

She said her life had been destroyed by her father's "evil and violent spirit". Kelly recalled: "I'd hear him killing me Ma all the time in the next bedroom. And I'd lie there with my hands over my ears just praying to

God he'd stop. He bashed me loads of times as well. When I was eight, he broke a tennis racket on my chin, and I had to get eight stitches. He did it because me and another girl were messing. He used to bash us for no reason at all. If you didn't do the dishes by the time he would tell you to, he'd kill you. Even his own mother said he was a violent person and a drug dealer. She brought him to St Brendan's [psychiatric hospital] at the age of eight and they said there was nothing wrong with him, that he was just an evil person.

"My Da had no friends, he was a bully. He bullied young boys and girls and took drugs off them. And if the guards arrived he would make me hold them so they couldn't arrest me. You don't do that to your children.

"And my poor mother is now in jail because she tried to protect me from that. She was not a bad person. My dad was the bad person and she only did it for me because my Da had me out selling drugs when I was thirteen. And he let me smoke hash when I was eight or nine.

"She did it for me basically and now she's being punished. She served life with him and now she is serving life without him."

Three years after Jacqui Noble's conviction, Kelly would also find herself standing in the dock, accused of manslaughter.

She had stabbed Emma McLoughlin to death and Kelly – who was now aged twenty-one – was facing a long sentence at the very same prison as her mother.

Kelly Noble had pleaded not guilty to the murder of nineteen-year-old Emma outside a shop in Laytown, County Meath, on 2 June 2006.

The grim two-and-a-half-week trial was a sorry tale of two deeply troubled young women.

Kelly Noble had been at home braiding her friend's hair when she decided to go to the local shop with one of her kids. Before going to the same shop, Emma McLoughlin had been drinking in the sunshine with her sister Shona, who said the alcohol had made her sister "happy", denying that Emma was a violent person when drunk.

Shona McLoughlin recounted the events: "They were rowing for a while and Emma was saying: 'Why did you hit me in the train station?' Then Emma hit Kelly and Kelly pushed her." Emma accused Kelly of kicking her in the stomach when pregnant. Emma was told to leave the supermarket and Kelly – no stranger to the gardaí – decided not to call for assistance. Instead, she phoned a friend of hers and asked her to bring a knife.

Kelly Noble's friend Niamh Cullen remembered getting the phone call: "She asked me to bring a knife down to Pat's shop and to come down and collect the children. I grabbed a knife, put it into a small schoolbag and hurried down to the shop." As Kelly Noble and Niamh Cullen tried to leave the shop, Emma McLoughlin again approached them.

Niamh Cullen said: "She [Emma] had Kelly, not pinned, but was in front of her stopping her from moving away from the window. Kelly and Emma started to shout at each other and the children started to cry. I was trying to get the children to calm down and not be looking at the two women."

As she tended to the children, she heard a thud and saw Emma McLoughlin lying on the ground. She never guessed that Kelly would use the knife. "Otherwise I would never have brought it," she said.

Kelly Noble had made good on a vow to one shop worker to "slice her up". Outside the shop, however, she had simply warned Emma McLoughlin to keep away from her. "She just lunged at me and the knife stuck in her," said Kelly.

Interviewed by gardaí, she said she never had any intention of killing that day and was afraid of getting her "head kicked in". "It was self-defence, big time," she told gardaí in a statement.

Gardaí were aware of the feud between the two women and in one previous incident Emma McLoughlin had attempted to attack Kelly Noble with a hammer.

The family of Emma McLoughlin said they never recovered from what happened. In her only interview, her mother Margaret described how she had been confined to a couch since her daughter died.

"Before Emma's death, I was well able to walk and work but since then, it has knocked the stuffing out of me," she said, speaking to the *Irish Sun*. "I can't come to terms with it. I have her here beside me and I pray for her every day, all day long."

Judge Barry White told the Central Criminal Court that Kelly Noble's crime was in the "upper range" of what constituted manslaughter.

However, her sorry family circumstances must have weighed heavily on his mind as he handed down a ten-year jail term, with the final two years suspended, accepting that Noble had had an "appalling upbringing". The sentence was later reduced on appeal to just six years and Kelly is likely to be free from prison in 2010. Her mother Jacqui will still be in jail, however, unlikely to be released until 2014 at the very earliest.

13

Declan Power: A Crime of Passion

The motive was no different to that of a hundred other crimes of passion these past generations in Ireland. It is one of the most ancient causes of murder – the jealous husband or wife who believes their partner has been unfaithful. Whether Joan Power was guilty or not of infidelity to this day remains a matter of conjecture.

After Declan Power first beat and stabbed his wife to death, then shot dead the man he suspected of being her lover, he gave himself up to gardaí. Phoning 999, he explained in halting words and through unstoppable tears that he had killed his wife out of jealous revenge and that her body could be found at the family home in County Waterford.

The forty-seven-year-old sincerely believed that his wife Joan and Mossie Curran, at whose pub Mrs

Power had previously worked, had begun an affair. Two days before he killed her, Joan Power – a mother of three children – made what her husband thought was a suspicious trip to Dublin to meet her sister. When Declan Power found out that Mossie Curran was in the capital at the same time, the fates of both of them would become for ever intertwined.

Garda Superintendent Michael Blake told Declan Power's trial that he had voluntarily given himself up, saying Power was "suspicious, jealous and possessive of his wife". "There was a confrontation when Joan Power returned from Dublin," explained the senior garda officer to a packed courtroom. "Declan Power killed her in an argument, striking her first with a rubber mallet and then stabbing her."

The exact time of the killing has never been made clear but in the early hours of Saturday, 9 March 2002, Declan Power had reached the end of his tether. He had been drinking heavily and in a haze of recrimination he confronted his forty-year-old wife. Joan had been working weekends with Mossie Curran in the pub he had bought two decades before, but just months before her death she had suddenly left to take up another part-time job in nearby Dungarvan.

It is not known how long Declan Power suspected his wife of infidelity but that night the dark suspicions that lurked in the back of his mind were made concrete.

By 2.50 a.m., Declan Power was at Decies Bar on Main Street, Clashmore, where his wife's boss and suspected lover lived. Mossie Curran, forty-eight years of age at the time, had earlier attended a darts match in Lismore and was alone in the pub at the time. Power confronted Curran and accused him of having an affair with his wife. The two men wrestled with each other and there was clear evidence of a fight inside the bar. What words were exchanged nobody will ever know. If Declan Power admitted that he had already killed his wife, only Mossie Curran ever heard.

The scuffle appeared to have ended; perhaps Curran thought the jealous husband had been chastened by the row inside the pub, but that dreadful night could only end one way. Instead, Declan Power went back to his car where he armed himself with a sawn-off shotgun before returning to the premises. Once inside, he fired off two shots in a rage, critically wounding Mossie Curran. The publican desperately tried to escape, dragging himself through the door and on to the street outside.

Declan Power followed him and in a final act of vengeance shot him one more time. Mossie Curran halted on the ground, fatally wounded by the three shots fired. One of the shots hit him in the face, garda sources said, although the post-mortem report was never released publicly.

Not long after he finished the publican off, Declan Power called his employer, who ran a local mechanic's firm, on his mobile phone. His boss convinced him to call the gardaí to confess what he had done. A call was logged by emergency services an hour later. By 5.00

a.m., gardaí were at the family home where they forced their way inside and found the dead woman on the floor of the living room.

Meanwhile, a taxi driver who had been working that night in Youghal, County Cork, was driving through Clashmore village when he came across Mossie Curran's body lying on the side of the road. It was just 3.05 a.m. and Declan Power had only left the scene, three shots having been heard at around 2.58 a.m.

The double killer was now effectively on the loose and checkpoints were put in place in both east Cork and west Waterford, where the two crime scenes were located. Ironically, the two murders would be investigated in separate garda regions, despite having taken place just a fifteen-minute drive apart, the result of a geographical quirk in the drawing of garda boundaries.

Despite his confession, Declan Power would not give himself up and remained a grave danger to himself and anybody who might get in his way. He was drunk, gardaí suspected, and driving his car wildly around the county, as every available squad car and even an Air Corps Alouette helicopter were dispatched to assist in the search.

Gardaí rang his mobile phone again, desperately trying to keep in contact with him, asking him to surrender even though the killer knew – with certainty – that he would spend a significant portion of his remaining years in jail. Declan Power refused to give in, and many officers involved in the early stages of the manhunt had resigned themselves to finding him dead in his car, his life snuffed out by the same shotgun that had killed Mossie Curran.

Gardaí continued to stay in contact, hoping against hope that this man – described later in court as a "model father and husband" – could be convinced to do the right thing, to give himself up and take whatever justice was coming.

Eventually, as the cold light of day began to dawn, Declan Power came to his senses and agreed to meet gardaí at a prearranged location. It was seven hours after Mossie Curran was shot dead when he finally handed himself over to gardaí at an abandoned farmhouse in Goat Island, around three miles from Ardmore. He came quietly and in tears, while the weapon he had used to murder the man he believed had cuckolded him was recovered nearby.

One local officer recalled: "The relief was palpable as we all knew that deep down we were dealing with an otherwise decent man. There were already two people dead and there was no need for another person to die. We knew he was armed and in the time between Mossie Curran's death and Declan Power's arrest, anything could have happened."

Two days later, Declan Power appeared in court charged with the murder of both his wife and Mossie Curran. He expressed his sorrow and extended his condolences to the Curran family, as he struggled to come to terms with what he had done to his own family and that of the other victim. "I want to express how awfully sorry that I feel for his wife and family," he said.

Told that he was being charged with the murder of his wife, he said just four words: "I am very sorry."

Sitting in court, impeccably dressed in a black suit and dark tie, the grey-haired mechanic was surrounded by family members, whilst a large crowd gathered outside the courtroom. His son and daughter hugged him in the court room while another daughter patted his face and fixed the lapel of his jacket, as tears ran down the side of her face.

At the funeral service for Mossie Curran, Clashmore parish priest Fr Maurice O'Gorman said: "Despite the deaths there has been no great anger on the part of any of the families directly affected. There was no rush to adopt blame, only a sincere wish to talk to each other and to share their grief.

"When death happens as tragically as these did, people are entitled to ask: Why us? Why our families? Why our community? But there are no answers.

"Mossie Curran had made the corner of the village where his pub was his own and he was so proud of what he had achieved there. Last Saturday, his body was lying in the wind and rain outside that same pub, it was remarkable that he should die at that corner," said the priest.

As he was buried, the coffin of the popular publican was draped in the red and green colours of his local Clashmore GAA club, where Mossie Curran had once played and served as chairman. He was mourned by his wife Veronica and his three children Eimear, Deirdre and Darragh.

In nearby Ardmore, on the very same day, the village came to a halt as an estimated 600 people gathered to pay their final respects to Joan Power, a "warm-hearted" woman who was popular throughout the locality.

Declan Power and his wife Joan had married in the 1980s and to all appearances seemed to have a happy life together. Joan had been working at Decies pub for the previous six years where she became close to Mossie Curran. He was a well-known businessman in the area and chairman of the local branch of the Vintners' Federation of Ireland.

According to friends of Joan Power, she had planned to leave her husband, tiring of his accusations, his jealousy and constant suggestions that she was having affairs with other men. She had left her job at Decies Bar at Christmas, hoping it might soothe her husband's concerns and convince him that she was not having an affair with Mossie Curran. Her sister had only recently moved back to Dublin and Joan Power was considering moving to the capital to stay with her, realising her relationship had reached breaking point.

Declan Power's legal team hired one of the country's most famous barristers, Patrick MacEntee, to defend him. He said that Power had been "devastated with remorse" since the killings and had been treated for depression and suicidal thoughts. Mr MacEntee said that Power was a hard-working man and a "loving and supportive father".

The garda superintendent who led the investigation, Michael Blake, said that the rest of Declan Power's family – including his three children Marie, John and Gemma – had continued to stand by him throughout their ordeal.

Gardaí, for their part, had little interest in hearing the private lives of Mossie Curran and Joan Power aired in public and kept their counsel when Declan Power agreed to plead guilty. As far as they were concerned, the two murders were solved and the perpetrator would face the mandatory life sentence. Their interest in the case ended there.

It was a peculiarly Irish trial, in that such a violent double murder could take place, and so little end up being known about it. In almost any other country, the minute details of the private lives of the three protagonists would have ended in the public domain, to be discussed and dissected at office water coolers around the land. Declan Power's statements of guilt, his confessions, the phone calls he made to gardaí in the early hours whilst on the run, the details of them all remain hidden.

The guilty plea drew a veil over the case, sparing his family and the loved ones of Mossie Curran yet more anguish. Details of the affair – whether it actually happened or not – will forever remain hidden, buried in a book of evidence in the Four Courts.

While the families attempted to put a brave face on it and a portrait of Declan Power as a man possessed by jealousy and revenge developed, the double killer's trial drew closer.

Judge Paul Carney had no choice, no option to show mercy towards a man who appeared utterly contrite, to take the mitigating circumstances into account. He sentenced Declan Power to two life sentences, both of which will run concurrently.

The convicted killer kept his composure even as his children broke down in tears – the sorry circle complete, their mother dead, their father destined to spend at least a decade behind bars.

Meanwhile, all of the families affected by the tragedy have done their best to move on, still trying their best not to let any enmity develop.

14

John Cullen: The Inferno

The blaze took hold at 4.40 in the morning. Two sisters, Kathleen Lynch and Hannah Hearne, were removed from the house covered in sheets, already dead, victims of an inferno they could never have escaped. Dolores Lynch somehow escaped alive, dragged to safety, only to die later that day at Dr Steeven's Hospital in Dublin's city centre. She had burns to eighty-five per cent of her body and the cause of death was listed as shock and pulmonary oedema. In court, a doctor described how they had to slice open her flesh to release the fluid.

Four units of Dublin Fire Brigade had barely managed to keep the fire from consuming more than just a single house at Hammond Street. Gardaí began routine forensic tests but they had no immediate reason to be suspicious. After all, who would want to kill two elderly women and a thirty-four-year-old hospital cleaner? Detectives had heard rumours that firelighters had been dropped through the letter-box of the home some weeks earlier but the theory of arson was discounted as merely local talk.

Dolores Lynch was no ordinary thirty-four-year-old, however. She had spent most of her early life working as a prostitute on the streets of Dublin. Before retiring from "the game", she had begun a campaign asking for a rehabilitation centre for the women who plied their trade on the streets around Benburb Street and the Grand Canal. She had written a letter to the Minister for Justice and had even written to then-President Patrick Hillery seeking assistance.

Dolores insisted that the seventy "girls" who risked their lives working as prostitutes on the streets were making life easier for ordinary women. "The women of Ireland couldn't walk the streets of Dublin in safety" if not for the women on the game, she famously declared.

By the time Dolores died, however, her prostitution days were a thing of the past and she had taken a job cleaning in the geriatric ward of a hospital. Gardaí had nothing to suggest a motive and Ms Lynch's association with the murky world of Dublin's red light district seemed like something from a far distant past. Besides, three women had died and if somebody had wanted to get at Dolores Lynch, surely there would have been an easier way than setting her mother's house alight?

Eleven days after the three women died, the garda investigation began in earnest when forensic tests returned results that suggested an arson attack was a very real possibility. The Garda Press Office confirmed that the deaths were now being treated as suspicious; they were even following a "definite line of enquiry".

The following day, John Cullen appeared in court. The unemployed Dubliner was charged with the murder of Dolores Lynch at Blackpitts on 16 January 1983. His partner, Elizabeth "Lyn" Madden, had come forward and had agreed to provide evidence on behalf of the State, beginning what would become the now infamous Blackpitts murder trial.

In 1976, Cullen had assaulted Dolores Lynch and was found guilty of wounding with intent to maim. He was given a two-year jail sentence and it was now the State's case that he had carried out the murder in revenge.

Lyn Madden was there on the night that he had deliberately started the blaze. In pre-trial hearings, the court heard how she and John Cullen had driven to the Blackpitts area of Dublin on the night in question. Madden, a former prostitute, was granted full immunity by the State in return for giving evidence about what had happened. She had been seeing John Cullen for about three years and dated him once or twice a week. When she was given a Dublin Corporation flat in Ballymun, he started to visit more regularly – almost every day.

Lyn Madden had known Dolores Lynch for about fifteen years and the two women had even lived together at one stage.

"He told me he was going to kill her for giving evidence against him. It was about seven years ago and he said she alleged he had asked for protection money," explained Lyn Madden. "She gave evidence against him in an assault case and he got three years. He said she would have to pay for depriving him of his wife and children. He had a number of ideas but they were all violent. He just wanted to make her suffer badly."

John Cullen had made two failed attempts to set the house on Hammond Street alight. On the first occasion, the fire went out and the second time, there were simply too many people around for him to go ahead with it.

On 16 January 1983, Cullen and Madden left the flat in Ballymun at around 3.30 a.m. When they arrived at Hammond Street, he first took a hammer, a butcher's knife and a Stanley knife from a hold-all and headed for the red-brick period house. The windows were opened and he returned. He took two containers of petrol from the car, each with a firelighter attached and four matches placed into each of the firelighters.

Cullen calmly asked Lyn Madden for two cigarettes and a cigarette lighter. He removed the filters of the cigarette and asked her to follow him down towards the house itself. He tried repeatedly to light the cigarettes but it was "breezy" and was proving more difficult than he had thought. "I could see a glow of flames but it kept going out," she said.

John Cullen walked towards the window of the house. "I could see flames shooting up," she said. "They seemed to go fairly high. I just ran away. He was still leaning in the window and I took it he was lighting up the second can. I was waiting for an explosion, so I ran.

"As I ran, I could hear glass breaking and a woman screaming. I kept running and John Cullen passed me out. He stopped and waited for me to catch up with him. As I caught up, he said: 'Did you see the smoke?' and I said 'No, I just heard the screams.' He hurried me along to the car."

They drove away from the scene at high speed and Cullen quickly discarded two rubber gloves which he had used. Later in the morning, Lyn Madden begged him to tell her what had happened.

"I will put it to you like this," he said. "Wait until you see the news tomorrow. If I have the right house you will know all about it. If not, well and good."

When they got to their flat, he stripped his clothes off and told her to wash them well. Cullen took his shoes and hers and dropped them down a rubbish chute in the high-rise flat complex where she lived.

Lyn Madden watched the television. That evening's news reported how three women had perished in a fire that was thought to have started accidentally. When Cullen arrived, she asked if he had heard the news. "Yes," he replied. "I am glad that she is dead." Later that night, she asked him again what he was feeling; he still said he was glad she was dead. They drove that evening to the beach at Portrane in north County Dublin where he tore up his clothing and threw it into the sea. On the drive back, they dumped the hold-all.

As Lyn Madden explained to the court what happened, she herself was accused of weaving a web of lies to guarantee her own immunity. Senior Counsel Barry White said: "I must suggest that whereas you may well be aware of the manner in which Dolores Lynch died and you may well have been involved in the firebombing of her house that night, it was not John Cullen but some other person involved with you."

White forced her to admit that she and Dolores had once argued over children's allowance. He said that John Cullen planned to leave her and that she had threatened to get her own back. "I must suggest to you", he said, "that the evidence you have given against Cullen is a tissue of lies."

Lyn Madden responded in her own inimitable style: "There is nobody only John Cullen crazy enough to do a thing like that. Can you suggest anybody else who would do it?"

Cullen seemed destined to go to jail. In interviews with gardaí, he even admitted his involvement, saying that he had never intended for three people to die. Interrogated by the then-Detective Garda PJ Browne, he said: "I thought they would make it out of the bed. I did not intend what happened. I did not want them dead."

He even exonerated Lyn Madden, saying she did not know where their intended destination was the night of the murders. "She would not be here only for me," he said. "I did not tell her where I was going. She would not have come with me if she knew it was Dolores Lynch's house. They were friends, but I hated her for doing the rat on me."

Prior to that, he had denied involvement, insisting that he was at his home in Kilbarrack that night. Cullen told gardaí he had been watching *The Late Late Show* and a doctor had walked off the programme. Detective Sergeant Timothy Hickey told him that incident had happened a month earlier. "He said he didn't care when it happened – he was saying he was in his own home on that night," explained the detective.

Cullen then claimed he had watched *Match of the Day* on television before retiring to bed. He got up at about 10.00 the next morning, by which time his wife and children had gone to Mass.

Grace Trimble, a friend of both Cullen and Lyn Madden, described how they had visited her flat the night after the murder. Trimble said that Lyn Madden had told her Cullen said he was glad about what had happened, saying that anyone who "rats" to the police deserves to die.

As the trial wound down, the jury rose to consider their verdict. Five hours later, they returned – one of the jurors was sick. The trial had to be halted and John Cullen's day of reckoning would be delayed.

A month later, Cullen was back in the dock. The damning dossier of evidence against him would be the same.

"He was very paranoid about her [Dolores]," explained Lyn Madden. "There was never a week but he didn't talk about her. He wanted to kill her because she grassed on him."

On the night of the fire, neighbours described how Dolores Lynch desperately tried to escape and begged for help for her elderly mother, who lay stricken in an upstairs room. The blaze had deliberately been started right underneath a staircase, ensuring there was no chance of escape except through one of the first-floor windows.

Sam Prendergast, a neighbour, described how he and another man had climbed up on to a roof at the back of the house and tried to pull Dolores Lynch to safety. As they tried to haul her out, she kept slipping from their grasp because her body had already been so badly burnt and blackened.

"I noticed she was very blackened," he said. "It was very hard to get a grip on her. She was sliding right through our hands. She kept asking us to help her mother – that is really all she was talking about."

The pathologist, Dr Sean O'Briain, told the court that Dolores had suffered eighty-five per cent burns to her body.

Fire officer Noel Hyland said it appeared to him as if the blaze had started away from the fireplace, on the stairs near a window.

A garda from Kevin Street station, Declan Mead, said on searching the scene that he had found three boxes of matches in the back yard and a book of matches near the back window. Inside, he found an intact firelighter, two pieces of coal and a shrivelled piece of plastic, the remnants of one of the petrol cans.

Lyn Madden, exhausted from the second trial, denied that she had done any deal in exchange for immunity, saying she would have been happy to go to jail.

"I'm sick and tired of everybody calling me a grass over this," she said. "There was no deal whatsoever. I did not know until March that I was not to be prosecuted. Furthermore, I didn't care if I was prosecuted. Three women died in the fire."

Turning to John Cullen, she said: "He set fire to it and he is sitting there laughing. The police didn't say anything about immunity. The only thing they guaranteed was protection. I've lived under a twenty-four-hour police guard for the past eleven months. I've had to have that to be able to be here to give evidence. Otherwise, I wouldn't be here. I'd be where Dolores is."

As the case wound down for a second time, the jury was told to put aside what they had heard about the sordid underworld of prostitution, pimps and crime. It was a simple case, ultimately, a question of whether they believed John Cullen or whether they believed Lyn Madden.

They chose the latter. John Cullen was found guilty of the murder of Dolores Lynch and of deliberately starting a fire at the house on Hammond Street. For the murder charge, he was given a mandatory life sentence and for arson he was given a further fifteen years in jail, with the two jail terms to run concurrently.

Justice McWilliam said: "This is one of the most serious offences that could be perpetrated, leaving aside the murder. The fact of setting fire to a house with people in it is simply appalling. I could not in a case such as this give less than fifteen years. The crime was committed without sympathy for anyone, or feeling of compassion."

Lyn Madden's life in Ireland was over and she was forced into hiding.

Hers was never destined to be a contented childhood. The family had been brought up in Cork, but Lyn's father Denny was a violent man. After getting a local thirteen-year-old girl pregnant, the father and the rest of the family fled to Dublin, to a workhouse in Capel Street. Whilst there, Lyn's brother Donny died and her parents split before Lyn and her mother took the boat to England.

She ended up in a convent school, Nazareth House on Hammersmith Bridge, when she was only seven years old. In a book she published about her experiences, she recalled walking into a large room with her mother Bridie and a nun. Her mother left the room, saying: "See you later" and the nun walked back in alone.

"Come on, Elizabeth," said the nun. "Take your coat off and I will take you to your dormitory."

Lyn disobeyed, refusing to take off her coat: "No, I'm waiting for mammy."

The nun replied: "Stop that at once. You are staying here. Your mother is not coming back. She doesn't want you. Now, take that coat off. Now."

Lyn was back with her mother at the age of eleven. At the age of fifteen, she left school, working at nineteen jobs, none of which she could settle into. A life of petty crime soon beckoned, beginning with the naïve theft of a cigarette lighter in a seaside village in her late teens.

From there, it was just a few steps to a life of prostitution and the day she was unfortunate enough to meet John Cullen.

Madden never had anything approaching what ordinary society might deem a normal life but in the decades since she helped send John Cullen to prison her life has been, if possible, even less ordinary. She lives under an assumed identity in the United Kingdom, for fear that revenge will once again come knocking on her door.

Lyn Madden has written two books about her experiences, the first simply titled *Lyn: A Story of Prostitution*, in which she recounted the damaged life that ended the day John Cullen roused her from her sleep in 1983. The book was a success, so successful that the publishers had to launch a newspaper appeal to find Lyn so that she could receive her unclaimed royalties.

The second book came more than twenty years later; entitled *Lyn's Escape*, it was effectively the story of what becomes of a woman who dares to give evidence against a dangerous man.

"You can go for hours without thinking about it, but then something small will remind you," she said in a rare interview to publicise the second book. "And you don't want to get past it. I'd feel terrible if I ever got over it, as if that meant it mattered less. Three people died and how could that not matter? It is twenty-five years but that doesn't lessen it and it's still as stark."

The appalling deaths of three innocent women in Blackpitts that night had a long-term impact on Irish society. It exposed the sordid underbelly of Dublin life, which had existed in notorious areas like Monto for as long as the city had. But it had been ignored and forgotten by official Ireland; the ever-present fact of prostitution swept under the carpet and deemed anathema to the devoutness of an overwhelmingly Catholic country. The girls who plied their trade on Benburb Street or around the Grand Canal were an embarrassment best ignored.

"I visited Dublin on a summer's day in 1987 and passed over Baggot Street Bridge. I was amazed at how lovely the Canal looks in day time," Elizabeth "Lyn" Madden wrote in her first book. "People strolled along the banks, and I doubt if any of them could have imagined what it was like at night . . . you never knew who was lurking in the shadows waiting to hurt you in some way. The game [prostitution] acts as a magnet for weirdos.

212

"Getting into a car was even more scary. Your heart raced as you assessed the client. And as you got in the car, you checked that it had a door handle on the inside and a window catch, in case you had to get out in a hurry. The silent ones were the worst."

15

Sara Neligan: A Victim of Circumstance

Sara Neligan was – at last – getting her life back on track. She had battled successfully against a drug problem and, to her family, it seemed like she was well on the road to recovery. She had a job working as a nurse in the Mater Hospital and on the outside, at least, appeared to be doing well.

Unbeknownst to them, however, Sara had landed herself in trouble again, this time purely by accident. She had met Brian McBarron on a trip to Waterford and from there the two had begun a relationship that was doomed to tragedy. Brian McBarron was a violent man but of that Sara Neligan had only the scantest of evidence. It became obvious to close friends that he occasionally beat her but the truth of just what he was capable of remained to them a mystery.

On the day that she died, Sara Neligan had been planning to leave him, planning to cast out on her own again, to attempt once again to put her life on an even keel.

Sara Neligan had not told Brian McBarron she planned to leave but he knew; a man as jealous and possessive as he could read the signs.

Around 9.00 a.m. on 14 June 2007, Sara had been expected to arrive in Gorey, County Wexford, on the 7.40 a.m. train from Connolly Station in Dublin. A friend, Martina Kehoe, had been expecting to meet her that morning and when she didn't turn up Martina knew that something was wrong. It was Martina who had noticed bruising on Sara's arms a month before the murder and convinced her to get out.

Martina rang Sara's mobile, and rang again. She continued to ring but there was no answer.

At 10.26 a.m., she got a call back from Sara's phone, but it was Brian McBarron on the line.

"She has a stomach upset," he said. "She is gone to the Blackrock Clinic."

Sara Neligan was never without her phone and something about McBarron's voice troubled her, warned her to expect the worst. She rang Sara's mother and managed to get the exact address for Sara's apartment at Pearse Street in Dublin's city centre.

She called the gardaí and explained what had happened. It was a routine call, one of many gardaí receive each day, but Martina Kehoe was convincing and would not take no for an answer.

At 10.50 a.m., gardaí arrived at the flat and tried to get in, but there was no answer. They returned to the station.

Brian McBarron phoned Martina Kehoe again, saying Sara was tired.

"She is in bed," he said. "She will call back when she wakes up."

There was no call. Martina Kehoe contacted gardaí again – twice at least – the desperation in her voice clear.

Gardaí returned to the apartment at 7.30 p.m. and spent more than half an hour trying to get in, but there was no response. Brian McBarron eventually came to the door.

"She is gone away for the weekend," he told them.

They persisted, asked to be allowed inside, to ensure that everything was okay. They explained that they had been phoned by a family member who was concerned for Sara.

"I have done a horrible thing," he confessed.

As gardaí stepped inside the flat, he led them towards Sara Neligan's body. Her favourite teddy bear had been placed in her arms but it did not cover the gaping wound in her chest.

She was face up on the bed and covered in blood. There were an indeterminate number of stab wounds. Her throat had also been slit.

"I wanted to die and I wanted to take her with me," said McBarron.

They had not argued. He had made a decision on their behalf; if he could not have her, then nobody could. Beside the bed, gardaí found a noose but McBarron had not had the courage to use it.

Brian McBarron's mother arrived that evening and accompanied her son to Pearse Street Garda station.

On the short drive there in a garda car, he admitted that he had killed her and that he had known she was on her way to Wexford that morning. What words were spoken between the two and how exactly he found out about her impending departure has never been revealed.

What is certain is that, as the prospect of the relationship ending loomed large upon him, McBarron lost control. He went to the kitchen and came back with a knife.

Sara Neligan was lying on the sofa some time around midnight when he grabbed her from behind and slit her throat. The wound would almost certainly have killed her but she put up a fight and managed to drag herself to the bathroom. Brian McBarron followed her, as the life seeped out of her, stabbing her again, a "good few times", as he put it in his own words.

The post-mortem carried out by State Pathologist Dr Marie Cassidy showed that Sara had suffered four serious wounds, any one of which might have killed her. The first was what she described as the "cut-throat" injury. Three other stab wounds had penetrated internal organs and arteries, two to the chest and one to the neck.

How long it took Brian McBarron to collect his thoughts, nobody will ever know, but collect them he did. He cleaned up the scene and undressed. He changed his clothes and threw away the bloodied items. Then, he went to a nearby shop where he bought a length of blue rope, the type used for making clothes lines. He had every intention of hanging himself and made the rope into a noose, which he hung from the ceiling.

According to gardaí, he later sat beside the body, talking to Sara, telling her he was sorry. "I just went out of my mind," he said.

CCTV footage had shown the couple going for dinner together at a nearby hotel the night before. Everything seemed normal and Brian McBarron seemed oblivious to the fact that Sara was about to leave him.

The next time he appeared on camera was the following morning, just after 2.00 a.m. He was carrying three large black plastic sacks – filled with his clothes – which he dragged to a large bin before dumping them.

When interviewed by gardaí, he estimated that he had spent at least an hour cleaning up. He had not done a particularly good job and gardaí arriving at the scene described being met with a blood bath. There was blood smeared across the walls and carpet. Sara's wounds were savage and the knife used to kill her was found in the apartment.

With the clothing recovered later by the detectives leading the hunt, blood from the victim and DNA samples from Brian McBarron were found. The evidence could have proved conclusive in the event of a murder trial but McBarron at least spared the Neligan family further heartache when he pleaded guilty to the killing.

When gardaí charged him with the murder, McBarron was contrite, saying simply: "I am deeply sorry for what I done."

In court, he asked his barrister to read a short statement expressing just how sorry he was about what had happened. "I wish to apologise to the family and friends of Sara for this brutal and thoughtless crime," he said. "She was a beautiful and talented young woman who had the whole world to live for and should not have died in the way that she died."

As the mandatory life sentence was handed down, McBarron said he hoped the punishment he was about to face would offer some comfort to them.

"I will live the rest of my life in shame and embarrassment," he said, before adding that he would gladly give his life in exchange for giving hers back.

The Neligan family, who avoided making any public statement about what had happened, gave thanks to all who had helped them "in this dreadful time" in a heartbreaking victim impact statement, read out at the trial. They praised the "thousands of people, many previously unknown to us, who stepped forward to offer their support in our hour of need. Many lent us the strength they had derived from similar tragedies. God bless you all. This family will never forget you."

They spoke about their Sara, the middle child of their family, "a beautiful, kind, caring and dignified young woman". "Her passing, long before her proper time, leaves us, her parents, sisters and brothers little consolation, save that of having known her. We shall take our cherished memories of her with us all the days of our lives until we meet again in a bright and happier place," they said.

Outside the court, solicitor Brendan Walsh – who was a close friend of the family – read out a statement on behalf of the family. "On behalf of Maurice and Patricia Neligan and their family, I have been asked to say that they are all very relieved that this process is now completed and whilst nothing can bring back their beloved Sara, they can at least now get on with their lives and move on.

"They want me to particularly thank all those in the process, particularly the gardaí and the prosecuting authority, for their careful and sympathetic handling of the case.

"They will not be commenting further or giving interviews and would ask particularly that their privacy would be respected."

Asked what he would say about Sara Neligan, he said: "I think that they [her parents and family] described her far better than I could."

The Neligan murder was just the latest in a long series of high-profile killings, where women were killed by the men they should have been best able to trust. There was Rachel O'Reilly, who was beaten to death by her husband Joe in the most notorious case of all. Then came Siobhan Kearney, who was strangled by her husband Brian, who then attempted to make it look as if she had taken her own life. There was Colleen Mulder, strangled by her husband Anton after years of an abusive relationship. These tragic crimes could not have been stopped; no level of policing could have saved those three women – trapped in marriages with secretly violent men. In several of these cases, the victim's only "mistake" was attempting to leave, to walk away from the abuse, to start anew.

What marked out the Sara Neligan killing, however, was that Brian McBarron already had convictions for serious violent crime. She knew nothing of it but on the night they first met in Waterford, McBarron should probably have been in jail.

He had five previous convictions, including criminal damage, driving offences and possession of a flick-knife. Despite having received a suspended sentence for another attack, McBarron had also threatened an ex-girlfriend with a flick-knife but could not be prosecuted for lack of evidence.

On 15 October 2006, he was arrested by gardaí after being seen drunk and brandishing a knife whilst living in a mobile home near Rathnew, County Wicklow, with his former partner. The couple had been drinking together in McBarron's home town of Arklow when the disturbance took place. Numerous witnesses reported seeing him on the street abusing her and wildly threatening her with a knife. She sought refuge in the pub until relatives came to take her away to safety. McBarron fled the scene before being arrested at the mobile home. He was found with the flick-knife but gardaí were only able to prosecute him for possession of the weapon. At Wicklow District Court, he admitted that he suffered from a serious drink problem and promised to get rehabilitation.

The incident with the flick-knife was not, however, the most serious offence on Brian McBarron's criminal record and he had already been given a suspended sentence for a knife attack on a barman. In December 2005, Sara Neligan's life could well have been saved had a two-year prison sentence handed down to Brian McBarron not been suspended.

The unprovoked attack on an Arklow street left the innocent barman with two cracked bones in his face. An account of the case in the *Wicklow People* from the time reported that McBarron was pleading guilty to the assault on Slovakian Martin Prokopec. Garda Marion Galvin explained how Prokopec was on his way home that night when he began a conversation with Brian McBarron, before offering him a cigarette.

As he headed home, McBarron demanded a second cigarette but Prokopec refused. McBarron caught up with him and attacked him with a knife, stabbing him several times in the face and head. He also suffered injuries to his abdomen, back and scalp. The wounds cut deep and tendons in his hand were left exposed, while he had broken bones in his eye and cheek. The twenty-six-year-old made an astonishing recovery from the attack but had since left Ireland and was now working in Scotland.

Using CCTV footage, gardaí quickly identified Brian McBarron – whom they knew as a violent man – as the culprit. When questioned by gardaí, McBarron again turned contrite, admitting he had drunk twelve cans of Carlsberg that night, which when mixed with the anti-depressant medication he was taking had caused him to turn violent.

He said he carried the eight-inch long blade he used in the attack for his own protection and that he had disposed of it after the attack. The garda witness said McBarron was "pleasant and quiet" unless he had taken drink.

Martha McBarron, his mother, said her son had not been well for more than five years. "With drink, he's like a monster," she said.

He had been treated in hospital in Newcastle but had since stopped taking his medication. He had promised his mother to stop drinking but in a chilling warning of what was to come, she said he was in urgent need of help.

Judge Pat McCartan handed down a suspended two-year sentence. If he offended again, the judge said, the sentence would be immediately reactivated.

After the flick-knife incident with his girlfriend, gardaí attempted to do just that and in May of 2007 they sought to have the sentence reactivated. McBarron had re-offended and just €5,000 of €10,000 supposed to have been paid in compensation had been handed over. The application was adjourned until July – a month too late for Sara Neligan. On 14 June 2007, she was stabbed to death, just hours before her new life should have begun.

The what-might-have-beens of Sara's life must be heartbreaking for her family.

What might have been had Brian McBarron's sentence not been suspended? Had he served the two years in jail without remission, he would have been behind bars on the night they first met in Waterford.

What might have been had gardaí been able to build a case against McBarron for brandishing a knife that day on Arklow's main street? Without certain witnesses, it was impossible.

What might have been had their application to have his sentence reactivated that day in May 2007 been successful? McBarron would have been where he belonged, off the streets, no longer a danger to anybody else.

Maurice Neligan, the world-famous heart surgeon, was Sara's father and whilst he did not publicly speak about his daughter's death, he wrote about her memory in his *Irish Times* column "Heartbeat" in September of 2007.

His were not words of revenge or of what-might-have-been, only of what-was and the beloved daughter that he remembered so fondly.

"Some days are better than others," he wrote. "Some days are forward looking with scarcely a backward glance. But the past comes unbidden, exposing our frailty and hurt. Such may happen unintentionally by those who wish only to assuage your loneliness and grief and may assume that you are far stronger than you really are.

"Yet such assertions of love and support and hope actually make your passage on the road that bit easier, knowing that you are not alone in your sorrow and that friends are there for us all at the difficult times."

The previous Wednesday, the staff and community of the Mater Hospital had held a memorial Mass to celebrate the life of Sara Neligan. Five of the Neligan family had worked in the hospital and Maurice and his wife Pat had married whilst employed as registrars there.

"I cannot adequately describe how deeply we were touched by the dignity and beauty of this occasion," wrote Dr Neligan. "We were strengthened and comforted by the loving and happy reminiscences of her colleagues who had known and worked with her during her all-too-short life.

"In this beautiful chapel, surrounded by ghosts of colleagues and sisters who had gone before and among them our little Sara, amidst the music and songs of hope, grief was not the motif, but rather the faith and expectation that is so important to us. We were touched, healed and inspired by you all."

Sara Neligan had spent her entire working life in the Mater Hospital, first as a student nurse and later as a staff nurse.

"We're very proud of the association," said Dr Neligan, "and the loyalty and love with which they remembered you, Sara, further strengthened the bond.

"I'd like to express our gratitude to the thousands of people who supported us through this time; many previously unknown, now friends for life. Known or unknown, close at hand or far away, we are grateful to you all and we will never forget."

16

Shan Mohangi: The Green Tureen Murder

Even against what might be considered the barbaric standards of modern criminals, this was still a murder of unspeakable horror. Shan Mohangi, a twenty-three-year-old South African medical student and part-time chef, stood in the dock accused of killing sixteen-year-old Hazel Mullen, a sometime model and bank employee.

Her dismembered body had been found chopped up at a restaurant on Harcourt Street in Dublin. An attempt had been made to incinerate the head and was only halted when neighbours spotted smoke billowing from a window.

The date was 21 August 1963 and Irish society, more used then to just a handful of mundane domestic and drunken murders each year, collectively gasped in horror as the young student was brought to court. As he stood charged with murder at his short initial hearing, Shan Mohangi looked dazed. His hair was dishevelled and he shook uncontrollably.

Superintendent Thomas Culhane took the stand to give evidence of how he had arrested Mohangi. "I told him who I was," he said, "and that I was taking him into custody on a charge of murdering one Hazel Mullen at 95 Harcourt Street, Dublin, at a time unknown between 12 noon on August 17 and 6 a.m. on August 20 and cautioned him."

Justice Patrick O'Grady asked Mohangi if he understood the charges. It was a time when any non-national appearing in an Irish court was a rarity. "Does he speak English?" asked the judge.

"He does – very well," replied Detective Superintendent Bernard McShane.

"I want it all over quickly," Mohangi had earlier told gardaí.

Within two months, the pre-trial hearings of Shan Mohangi would begin and transfix an Irish public, which listened in astonished awe at how a beautiful young Irish girl could be dismembered with a carving knife and a meat cleaver.

During the next year, Mohangi would be found guilty of murder and sentenced to death, only to have that conviction overturned. Mohangi, who was studying medicine and was the son of an Indian plantation owner then living in Natal, South Africa, had planned to marry Hazel Mullen.

Mohangi began his statement to gardaí by describing how he had come to Ireland to study medicine at the Royal College of Surgeons in Dublin. In September 1961, he had met a girl and gone out with her for six months. She had been working in Dublin but subsequently gave up her job to return to the country.

"We corresponded for a while and then stopped," he said. "About five months after this girl left town I met another girl, Hazel Mullen, about August 1962. She was working in Brown's chemist shop in St Stephen's Green.

"I have been taking her out regularly since then and every weekend and sometimes after work I took her out to her home at St James' Lodge, Crinken, Bray [County Wicklow]. Last Christmas, I stayed for about a week at her home."

Four months later, the couple argued about whether they should get engaged. Hazel Mullen's mother believed they should wait until she had turned seventeen, but Shan Mohangi was "very jealous" of her and wanted her to himself.

Mohangi said he had always been incredibly possessive. He had long believed that he had been her only boyfriend and when she disclosed one evening that she had once kissed another man, he had hit her a "clout".

"I regretted it and told her that I was sorry," he said.

They spent the rest of the evening together before Mohangi dropped her home to Bray, where he admitted to Hazel's mother that he had punched her.

Unfazed by this first sign of violence, the couple began to spend even more time together and he described how, during holidays, he would visit her every single day.

When Hazel was doing some part-time modelling at the Horse Show in the RDS, he would bring her out for lunch each day. The couple again discussed their engagement, with Mohangi saying: "Your Mammy won't refuse us this time."

By this time, Hazel's mother Bridget trusted Mohangi. She explained to the murder trial: "I had a private talk with him and told him that Hazel . . . had never been out with boys. I told him she knew nothing about the facts of life. I gave him permission to take her out on condition that he would take good care of her."

The Saturday that she died, Hazel Mullen called over to Shan Mohangi at Harcourt Street where she asked to be shown around the restaurant, which was downstairs from the flat where he lived. "I brought her down and showed her all over the basement," he said. "We hugged and kissed each other in the basement. She told me in the basement that she had something to do with somebody else."

"She did not mention the person's name", he said, "but she said it was sex," he confessed to gardaí in a statement.

"I don't know what happened to me. I always loved and worshipped her for that one thing. At least I thought she was different, something special, but she was a mere disappointment to me. I had been prepared to give up everything at home, including my parents for her, and yet she had let me down."

As he spoke to the investigating officers, he carefully considered every word, recalling in intricate detail what had happened, how she had paid for her infidelity, how he had been overcome by anger and vengeance.

"I don't know what happened to me," he said. "I got a hold of her and put my hands around her neck and before I knew anything it was the end."

Mohangi was "raging"; he grabbed her by the throat and strangled her. She made a vain attempt to fight back but the man who said he loved her was too strong.

He said that he then panicked and ran up the stairs, leaving the body lying there on the floor, hoping against hope that he had not killed her. He said: "I came back down in a short time and I saw that she was dead. I cut up the body and hid it. I was panicky all the time. I was afraid to give myself up to the guards."

The day after the murder, Mohangi invited Hazel's brother Desmond and his girlfriend to enjoy dinner at his home. He served them roast chicken in his upstairs flat. The young student then went downstairs where he worked his normal four-hour shift in the Green Tureen restaurant. Hazel's mother, who by this stage trusted Mohangi implicitly, called him and asked if he knew where she was. Mohangi somehow managed to keep his cool and explained that he had no idea where Hazel was.

The following day, when she hadn't turned up, Desmond Mullen and Shan Mohangi went to Shankill Garda station where they reported a missing woman. It was late that evening and Mohangi stayed the night at the Mullens' home in Bray from where the search would start again the following morning. There was no sign of Hazel Mullen the following day and Shan Mohangi again stayed the night in her family home.

On Tuesday morning, the South African turned up at the Green Tureen for work as normal before resuming the search that night. It was fully three days after the murder when Shan Mohangi finally confessed his involvement to his landlord Cecil Frew. He owned the property on Harcourt Street and had employed the medical student as a commis chef in the restaurant downstairs.

The two men had previously discussed Hazel and Mr Frew had suggested that he concentrate on his studies. That night, he had something to get off his chest.

They were driving around Dublin, ostensibly searching for the missing woman, when Mohangi said: "I am in trouble, will you help me?"

"I said: 'Is it about the girl?' He said: 'Yes.'

"I asked him: 'Is she dead?' He said: 'Yes.'

"I asked him: 'Is she in the building?' He said: 'Yes.'

"I told him that what he had said put me in a certain position . . . I told him that he would have to face up to this and that he could not run away from it."

Mohangi confirmed this to gardaí: "I told my landlord . . . that the girl was dead and the body was in his house. I believed he would tell the guards. I was afraid to face the general public, as everybody speaks quite highly of me, and I was ashamed to show myself, so I decided to dispose of myself."

Mohangi took an overdose of tablets, turned on a gas cooker, placed his head inside and waited for death. His suicide attempt failed; he was rushed to hospital and eventually came to. As soon as he awoke, he began crying hysterically and had to be secured to a couch using straps.

Doctors certified him as fit and he was taken into garda custody as a forensic examination of the building took place. Detective Superintendent Patrick McLoughlin said that the basement appeared to have been used as a store, filled with bags, dustbins, boxes and other rubbish. Behind a large piece of plywood, he found pieces of a dismembered female body. The head of Hazel Mullen was missing.

In an adjoining cellar, he found a large carving knife and a meat cleaver on a bench. Smeared along the passageway between the two rooms was what appeared to be blood. He went to Mohangi's flat on the top floor of the building where he saw a sheet of cardboard reading: "Everything belonging to me goes to Josephine Farrelly [his former girlfriend]."

Detective Superintendent McLoughlin returned to Harcourt Terrace Garda station where he joined the interrogation of Shan Mohangi. The young student agreed to cooperate but some details of his crime, he insisted, must not be included in his statement.

"Some of the deceased's clothing was burned and the liver and intestines are gone out in the bin," the garda officer wrote. When he asked Mohangi where Hazel Mullen's head had gone, the young student insisted that it was with the rest of the body.

He described to them where Hazel's umbrella and handbag were, helpfully drawing a sketch of the building. Asked where the clothes in which he had killed her were, he said: "My own trousers are at the back of the gas meter at the top landing."

Detective Superintendent McLoughlin returned to the Green Tureen restaurant where he found the hidden items and, behind a service hatch, a pair of lady's shoes, a blood-stained blouse and a pyjama top.

Two hours later, another garda involved in the search made a grim discovery, spotting what appeared to be human flesh hidden behind an asbestos sheet. When the asbestos panel was removed, five pieces of Hazel Mullen's body tumbled out.

A horrified jury at his murder trial heard that Mohangi had put Hazel's head in the oven and set the heat on full so that, when discovered, it was unrecognisable. The twelve men and women were shown photographs of the partially incinerated head, internal organs discovered in a refuse bin and other body parts, which had been hidden around the building. The State

Pathologist, Professor Maurice Hickey, said that it appeared as if the head had "been roasted". There were no signs of a struggle on her fingers or fingernails, he said.

Crucially, parts of Hazel Mullen's body were never found. Mohangi's defence had used the possibility of a condition called "vagal inhibition" which would have given a possible explanation of how she had died with only a small amount of pressure on her neck. Catching a man by the throat with the intention of scaring him could even cause his death, the State Pathologist said. It was, however, never possible to fully determine whether this had in fact happened as the whole front of her throat, including her voice box, had been cut away and was never recovered. Other bodily organs were also missing, which made determining the exact cause of death virtually impossible.

Professor Hickey said it was not even possible to exclude the possibility of death from natural causes with only parts of a body to examine. He said the brain was in no condition for a medical examination and the important internal organs were all missing. Death could have been caused by cutting the throat or by stab wounds in the abdomen or heart, he told the court, but the heart was missing so he could not say for certain. Suffocation or strangulation could of course have been to blame but it simply was not possible to tell.

Mohangi's trial was never a question of guilty or not guilty; it was simply a question of murder or manslaughter. Even today, the distinction is huge and can mean the difference between fifteen years in prison or a much shorter jail term of perhaps seven years. But in Shan Mohangi's time, the stakes were much higher: the death penalty was still on the books and, if found guilty, the South African would face hanging.

On 22 February 1964, Mohangi became the last non-political prisoner ever to be sentenced to death in Ireland. Asked if he had anything to say, he replied: "I have nothing to say, my Lord."

Papers for an appeal were lodged within days and the conviction was thrown out by the Court of Criminal Appeal. There were a number of grounds of appeal and the original trial was ruled unsatisfactory, chiefly because certain evidence should have been excluded. Mohangi had escaped the noose and a grim date of death with the famous executioner Albert Pierrepoint.

By June of 1964 Mohangi was back on trial for murder. After six days, he was found innocent of murder but guilty of the lesser offence of manslaughter. Newspapers from the time recall how the second trial did not attract the same level of interest as the first. During the original hearings, the court gates had to be locked to prevent members of the public from overcrowding the galleries.

Shan Mohangi's lawyers appealed for leniency, saying their client's life in Ireland had been ruined and that his prospects on returning to South Africa were little better.

The judge responded by saying the killer had "desecrated the corpse" and in doing so had destroyed much of the evidence of the assault. Some of the body parts had never been found and Hazel Mullen's family had been forced to bury her dismembered body without a heart. For the "aggravated manslaughter", he handed down a seven-year jail term.

Shan Mohangi had the chance of again appealing his conviction and sentence but upon appearing in court again he decided to accept his punishment. Four years later, he was a free man, released from custody on 11 April 1968. He returned to South Africa.

His death sentence led to a sea-change in Irish opinion, which was already turning away from the ultimate sanction of hanging. Over the course of two trials, the public-at-large watched a distraught Mohangi explain how he had killed his love in revenge for her past indiscretions. Nobody forgave him the crime but the punishment seemed too severe. Taking his life would do nothing to bring back Hazel Mullen. The case would eventually culminate in the scrapping of capital punishment except for offences including treason and the murder of a garda or a judge.

In 2009, the past of Shan Mohangi – now living back home in South Africa under the name of Narentuk Jumuna – came back to haunt him yet again.

Mohangi had been running in the South African elections as a candidate with the small Independent Democrats party. A report in the *Saturday Star* newspaper disclosed that Narentuk Jumuna was in fact the same man who had strangled Hazel Mullen in Ireland in the 1960s. He had changed his name immediately on returning to South Africa following his release from prison.

Since his return to Natal, he had become a successful farmer and businessman. As far as Mohangi is concerned, he has done his best to make amends for the past. He still insists that he never had intentions of killing Hazel Mullen and that his solitary moment of madness has blighted his life since.

In one interview with the *Mail on Sunday*, he said: "My greatest wish now is to be allowed to return to Ireland and to somehow make recompense for the terrible thing I did and to find closure for myself."

Mohangi's "outing" as a convicted killer was in fact no such thing and the South African farmer and businessman had been open about his past. He had even appeared on an RTÉ programme to discuss the murder and to again offer the best apology he could make.

The young medical student, who had left Ireland a convicted killer, had even served during the apartheid era as a parliamentarian in the House of Delegates. And the Mullen family held absolutely no ill-will towards him. On hearing that he was planning to run as an MP in 1984, Bridget Mullen released a statement saying: "If Shan is worthy of success in business and politics, I bear no grudge and wish him well."

Hazel Mullen's brother Ian also said the family had forgiven him. Speaking on RTÉ, he said: "Not only have we forgiven Shan, but in our view God has forgiven him. Therefore, he has a clean slate and every right to run for office. Who are we to judge anybody? None of us can judge another man."

For Shan Mohangi, however, there is only the realisation that contrition is never enough in today's society.

"Hazel was a special girl," he recalled. "Her folks were real down-to-earth, working-class Irish people. Her mother was a widow who had converted to the Church of Ireland when she married and now the whole family lived in a church lodge.

"Hazel and I didn't have much money, so we did simple things, visits to the cinema and long walks up to Killiney Hill where we would talk and cuddle for hours on the lovers' seat up there, overlooking the city and the wonderful Wicklow Mountains."

Mohangi, to this day, admits he was far too possessive of her, that he was a jealous young man far from home. "I realise now that I had formed an unrealistic and passionate attachment to Hazel, a forceful possessiveness, which ended in tragedy," he said.

Looking back on those days, Shan Mohangi says he was consumed by a kind of madness, living in a blur in the days following the murder when he first chopped up her body and then joined the search party. "When I look back, I can't believe it was me who killed her. I never meant to end her life. I was in a blind, hysterical, shock-induced panic, that's all I can say."

Mohangi said he had accepted his fate and was willing to die at the end of the hangman's noose in Mountjoy Prison. He spent a month on death row. "I was sentenced to death by hanging," he said. "I did not care about that. I had no feeling except that I had done wrong and I was being punished. I was calm and I accepted my fate."

Shan Mohangi says he remembers little of those days in prison but astonishingly Hazel's mother Bridget visited him repeatedly, accompanied by a preacher. He recalled: "We prayed together. We prayed for Hazel and we prayed for me. I am not a religious man but I believe in one true God. The Mullen family's kindness and prayers got me through."

17

Christopher Crowley: You Will Never See Her Face Again

If Christopher Crowley could not have his daughter Deirdre, then as far as he was concerned, nobody could.

For close to two years, Deirdre's mother Christine O'Sullivan had made appeal after unheard appeal desperately seeking information on the whereabouts of her by then six-year-old daughter. At every opportunity, she would speak to newspapers or give interviews on radio or television in a vain attempt to track down her smiling little girl.

Christine O'Sullivan had even travelled to the United Kingdom, certain that Christopher Crowley had fled Ireland to parts unknown with their daughter. In actual fact, Crowley was less than sixty miles from her front door in Cork, living under the radar in a rented house in Clonmel, County Tipperary.

For gardaí, the trail appeared to have run cold with the discovery of Christopher Crowley's car at a hotel near a ferry port in Wexford and their long-standing assumption was that he had left the jurisdiction.

For the media in Ireland, Christine O'Sullivan's case was one in which they thought they were of limited use. Endless appeals for information yielded virtually nothing but hopeless leads and nobody for a minute suspected Crowley was still in Ireland.

The abduction of a child would under ordinary circumstances have captivated the Irish public – but when the kidnapper was the father, the normal rules did not apply.

Twenty-one months later, a tip-off combined with telephone monitoring led gardaí to an area on the outskirts of Clonmel where Crowley had quietly made himself a bolt-hole. Under the guise of carrying out an investigation into rogue builders, gardaí began to carry out house-to-house inquiries, unsure of the exact location but certain that the missing father and daughter were nearby.

They rapped on the door of Croan Lodge and Christopher Crowley answered. His behaviour certainly seemed suspicious but the gardaí involved needed to confirm that they had found their man.

When they approached the home again a short time later. Crowley must have been watching through a window. As they closed in on the door, gardaí heard a low muffled sound – the blast of a shotgun from the back of the house.

REVENGE

Crowley had exacted the ultimate revenge on his former wife, taking away the only thing she had to live for.

The sorry saga had begun on 4 December 1999 when Crowley, who had separated from his wife a year earlier, arrived to take Deirdre for a night. It was a routine visit, one of countless that he had already made, access that had been agreed upon after the separation.

Christopher Crowley and Christine O'Sullivan were both teachers. He taught French and Maths at a secondary school in Fermoy, County Cork while she worked as a lecturer in the Cork, Institute of Technology. Deirdre was born in 1995 but three years later the couple had split. The break-up had not been particularly acrimonious and Christopher Crowley had plenty of access to his child. On Christmas Eve, for instance, Deirdre would spend the day with her father before returning to her mother in Cork the following morning.

The day of the abduction, Christopher Crowley's willingness to cooperate had finally been exhausted. He decided he would take his daughter away, something that he had been planning for up to six months.

He drove his daughter first to a hotel car park in County Wexford, where he abandoned his car, determined to give the impression that the father and daughter had been foot passengers aboard a ferry bound for the UK or France departing from Rosslare.

When they didn't return that night, Christine O'Sullivan rang her former husband and asked him where he was. He replied that he would return the following day but he didn't come back that evening, or the next evening, and Deirdre Crowley was never seen alive again by her mother.

From the beginning, the case was characterised by what appeared to be a malaise in both the garda investigation and the media campaign to find Deirdre. Christine O'Sullivan tried desperately to keep her daughter's face in the public eye but, like all long-running disappearances, newspapers and broadcasters eventually tire of the story and it fades from view.

Sergeant Brian Fitzgerald of Douglas Garda station, where the original investigation was based, summed it up best at the time, saying: "If a four-year-old girl was taken by a stranger, the whole country would be up in arms. Because it was her father, people don't seem to be as concerned. They say that the case is sad, but tend to think that she is safe with her father."

And for twenty-one months, little Deirdre Crowley *was* safe with her father, a man who was to all appearances a pillar of society. Their planned disappearance remained undiscovered, not least because they had the help of a number of willing accomplices.

During the two years in which they were on the run, Deirdre Crowley barely set foot outside the doors of the remote cottage in County Tipperary where her young life would eventually end. Neighbours hardly knew them and forty-three-year-old Crowley went by the false name of Mr Allen. His rent was paid on time and he lived a quiet life; nobody had any reason to disturb or call on him.

One regular visitor to the house, however, was Regina "Gina" Nelligan, with whom the then twenty-six-year-old Christopher Crowley had formed a relationship when she was a teenage student of his at a school in Fermoy, County Cork. The liaison began during a school trip to Paris and continued until after she had completed her Leaving Certificate. They holidayed together in Italy before splitting when Regina Nelligan moved to Dublin, where she studied at the National College of Art and Design.

The relationship eventually ended but at some undetermined point contact had resumed and, in July 1999, they made an arrangement to meet in a car park in Portlaoise, where they began to hatch the outline of the abduction plan.

Ms Nelligan first made arrangements to organise accommodation in Clonmel, where Christopher Crowley and Deirdre lived during their disappearance. On 4 December, the day Deirdre Crowley vanished, Regina Nelligan met her former teacher in the car park of the Talbot Hotel in County Wexford. The car was abandoned as planned and they drove together to Clonmel.

Regina Nelligan continued to visit the cottage as often as she could escape from work in Dublin, bringing food and other supplies. She made contact with Crowley's friends, using a prearranged code, to tell them that both father and child were safe. Unbeknownst to her, in the weeks leading up to the tragedy, gardaí had been monitoring calls from phone boxes near her home and were beginning to determine a pattern.

Her trial heard that Christopher Crowley had cashed an insurance policy worth IR£17,000 and taken out another loan for IR£10,000 before he had abducted his daughter. He had made plans that the money raised from the home he had shared with Christine O'Sullivan would pass to his family and friends.

When the investigation into Deirdre Crowley's abduction was in its early stages, gardaí had actually called to Regina Nelligan's home in Dublin. She claimed to have no contact with Crowley any more and claimed they had fallen out on the trip to Italy.

Suspicions were further aroused, however, when newspaper articles about the case were found in her home, but Nelligan said she was just curious about what had become of her former teacher. Detective Sergeant John O'Driscoll, who was then working with the National Bureau of Criminal Investigation, interviewed her at the time. "What type of person do you think I am?" she said. "If I knew where the child was I would tell you."

Nelligan, garda sources admitted, had been blinded by love and loyalty. Christopher Crowley claimed that he had removed Deirdre from her mother for the child's own protection and she had foolishly believed him. He had lied and claimed that Christine O'Sullivan was suffering from chronic post-natal depression and was not in a fit state to care for Deirdre.

At Regina Nelligan's trial, Christine O'Sullivan was forced to defend her own reputation as a mother, saying her daughter had been "a gift". "When she was born, she was so beautiful; she was just so incredible; such a gift. For nine months, I breastfed her and I cared for her at all times," she said.

Remembering the day she had last seen her daughter's face, she said: "I hugged and kissed her goodbye. I had no way of knowing that I would never see that gorgeous little face again and that twenty-one months later it would be shattered by a shotgun blast. This could have been prevented by so many people."

Nobody can ever know how long the arrangement could have continued. Deirdre Crowley was all but a prisoner in her own home, with no friends, no schooling and no conception of what had become of her mother.

There had just been a single reported sighting of the two of them actually out and about in Clonmel, nine days before they were eventually found dead, and even that did not emerge until after the killings. A shopkeeper in the town, Eddie Kelly, had described how he saw the two of them in Hearn's Hotel sitting together.

"What caught my attention," he told *The Irish Times*, "was that they only had one cup of coffee, which he was drinking, and there was nothing else placed on the table. They were talking away.

"He was smiling at her with a very soft smile. I found it extraordinary the way he kept smiling at her. I found it unusual as well that she was not having anything to eat; but then I thought she had probably had breakfast at home and they had just called in because he wanted a coffee."

Neighbours did not even know that there was a little girl in the house at the time. The local milkman said he had never seen a child there and some local residents actually believed the house was unoccupied altogether. Besides, the house was relatively isolated. There were new occupants at the house closest to it and they probably never thought twice about the reclusive man next door.

There was a time in Ireland when a father and young daughter moving into a cottage on the outskirts of a town like Clonmel would almost certainly have aroused a degree of curiosity. At some point, somebody would surely have joined the dots and connected this strange and quiet man to the girl whose beaming smile still cropped up from time to time in the daily newspapers. For whatever reason, be it chance or negligence, those dots were never joined and it would take an anonymous tip-off to gardaí to uncover Christopher Crowley's secret life.

Chief Superintendent Pat O'Boyle, who led the investigation, said that gardaí had become suspicious of the "male occupant" of the house while carrying out inquiries at around 3.15 p.m. on the day of the murder. He said: "Gardaí left the scene to make further inquiries and subsequently returned to the vicinity of the house and while approaching the home heard a muffled sound, which caused them concern.

"Failing to gain entry, they forced their way into the house and found the bodies of a middle-aged male and a young child, aged approximately five to ten years, dead in the house."

Gardaí have still failed to clarify officially whether they were in fact carrying out routine inquiries regarding what were supposed to be rogue builders or whether they had definitive information about Christopher Crowley. A subsequent inquiry into their handling of events was delivered to the Garda Commissioner and the Minister for Justice but, like all internal police inquiries in Ireland, its findings were never published.

The gardaí who made their way into the house will never forget what they saw. The first detective on the scene refused to let a colleague into the room because what was inside was so horrific.

Not for a second did gardaí ever suspect that Christopher Crowley would harm his daughter but during the twenty-one months he had spent on the run, his mental state had deteriorated. Crowley had obtained a shotgun, stolen from a shed in his former school in Fermoy. He had also got his hands on forty cartridges for the weapon, suggesting that he never intended being taken without a fight.

The cottage contained large stockpiles of food so that the father and daughter could survive for long periods of time without ever opening their front door.

When the State Pathologist, Dr John Harbison, arrived at Croan Lodge, he found a neat and well-kept home with food freshly prepared in the kitchen. There were toys – including dolls and teddy bears – stored in boxes along with crayons, pastels and a bottle of kid's cough medicine on the mantelpiece.

Two shotgun cartridges had been left sitting on a sofa and in a small utility room the body of Christopher Crowley lay partly slumped across little Deirdre Crowley. Crowley's hand was wrapped around the barrel of the shotgun and the thumb of his other hand remained lodged against the trigger. Deirdre was wearing a vest and blue shorts with sandals and socks.

Professor Harbison described at the inquest how Crowley had first shot his daughter before taking his own life.

Deirdre died instantly. She had been shot at close range and the pathologist was "at a loss" to explain two bruises on her neck. She had suffered catastrophic injuries to her head and not a single part of her face was recognisable after the shooting. The traumatised gardaí involved in the case often asked themselves why he couldn't at the very least have shot his beautiful daughter in the body. One officer said: "I always felt it was his last two fingers to his wife, him saying you are never going to see or touch her face again. People say that he loved his daughter but those moments that he stood over his daughter with a shotgun in his hand are beyond human comprehension."

Professor Harbison said that Crowley had shot himself in the side of the neck and cheek. His skull was intact, however, and it appeared as if he had not died instantly. Perhaps, one garda involved later speculated, he had reconsidered at the last second. He survived for perhaps a couple of minutes, eventually succumbing to shock and the blood loss caused by the gunshot wound. He had been wearing a tracksuit and in the pockets were little bobbles that he used to tie up Deirdre's hair.

On the day that Deirdre Crowley died, gardaí had made contact with Christine O'Sullivan to say tentatively that they may have found her daughter.

"I just don't believe it," she said the day after the tragedy. "It hasn't sunk in yet. I can't believe that I won't see my baby again, especially when we were so close to finding her. I thought I was going to be holding her in my arms this evening and cuddling her and telling her how much I missed her and telling her how hard I worked to try to find her."

For Christine O'Sullivan, there would be no further answers, no real closure, no opportunity to ask her former husband what was going through his mind when he destroyed her life.

She was not the only casualty. Regina Nelligan, once a smitten young student at Loreto College in Fermoy, ended up in prison, guarded in a protection wing for fear she would be attacked by other inmates.

In January 2003, she pleaded guilty to abduction as her legal counsel told the court how she was undergoing ongoing psychiatric treatment and evaluation. A month later at a sentencing hearing, Nelligan was given a two-year term in jail, with the last six months suspended.

Judge Michael O'Shea specifically highlighted the number of times Christine O'Sullivan had made public appeals for information, and how she had used special occasions like birthdays, Christmas and the anniversary of the abduction in a vain attempt to elicit some cooperation. He said Regina Nelligan had played a key role in organising the accommodation in which Deirdre Crowley was kept a virtual prisoner and that she had done everything possible to keep that location secret.

Her barrister Niall Durnin said that Christopher Crowley had exerted a "dominion" over Regina Nelligan, not unlike the grasp that child abusers have over their victims.

Judge O'Shea responded: "Chris Crowley was her first boyfriend and, in her view, was perfect and she was madly in love with him.

"[However] Deirdre Crowley was deprived of a basic human right – the right to a childhood – over the two-year period, the right to go to school; the right to play with other children . . . [while] the love, affection and guidance of her mother Christine were also denied her."

As far as Christine O'Sullivan was concerned, her young daughter may as well have been in prison. She recalled walking through the rooms of Croan Lodge, looking at mildewed sheets and the TV and video player, in front of which Deirdre Crowley must have sat for endless days.

"The people who obstructed me in my efforts to get Deirdre back have an awful lot to answer for," she said. "Chris's plan would never have succeeded had it not been for the help he got. So many people knew and did nothing."

In the final interview she gave in 2004, before attempting to return to a life away from the search for her lost daughter, Christine O'Sullivan said: "Sometimes, I have nightmares that Chris is chasing Deirdre and me and I can't protect her. Sometimes, I fall asleep and dream that Deirdre is in my arms. I am kissing and cuddling her. Those are the best dreams. It is very hard to wake up and find they are not real."

She said that Christopher Crowley had deliberately shot his daughter so that she would be unrecognisable, the *Irish Mirror* reported. "He was determined I would never look into my beautiful girl's face again, even in death."

18

Deborah Hannan and Suzanne Reddan: When Life Does Not Mean Life

The ferocity of the attack on Tracy Butler was such that gardaí initially assumed the culprits must have been two men.

Pathologist Dr Margaret Bolster described her findings to a shocked jury, explaining how the seventeen-year-old was the victim of a brutal and sustained assault, suffering fourteen stab wounds to her neck, chest and arms, and thirty-five other injuries including cuts and bruises across her body. Her brain had even swollen after the attack. The main injuries were three separate knife wounds to one of her lungs, which caused the collapse of her left lung and two of her arteries.

Two knives – a carpet knife and another domestic knife with a serrated edge – were shown to the pathologist, who said the serrated knife could have been used to inflict the fatal wounds. The carpet knife could not have been used to kill her because the blade was too short and the wounds that caused her death were far deeper. It could, however, have been used to inflict the more superficial cuts to her face and other areas, she said.

Dr Peadar McGrath, on duty the night when Tracy Butler arrived in the emergency room, described how he had helped in the resuscitation attempt but that little could be done considering the severity of the injuries. The official cause of death was listed as shock and haemorrhage due to collapsed lungs caused by multiple stab wounds.

Tracy Butler never stood a chance; her "crime" was to have witnessed the brutal killing of William Hannon ten days before her own death. As Hannon lay dying on the ground, Tracy Butler was reported to have sniggered and mocked the stricken man.

His daughter Deborah Hannon was intent on revenge and on 12 July 1993 decided she would take the law into her own hands. Ms Hannon, just eighteen at the time, waited for Tracy Butler as she walked home from a night out with friends. Hannon was accompanied by twenty-five-year-old Suzanne Reddan, who had been in a relationship with the dead man. Reddan had cradled William Hannon as he died after a brutal assault with weapons including a plank and a sewer rod. As she knelt there, talking to her lover, begging him to stay alive, a crowd gathered around her, mocking and jeering, laughing at her tears. Tracy Butler was a part of that crowd.

Tracy had gone to visit a friend at O'Callaghan Avenue in Limerick city on the night she died. Leaving the house at about 11.30 p.m., the only words she would ever speak again were her dying words, begging for help, struggling to draw breath.

Witnesses described hearing terrified shouting from the Ballynanty Road and two people, wearing dark clothes and hooded, fleeing the scene. One eyewitness, Edward McCarthy, described how he had seen two hooded figures attacking the teenager on the street. He heard Tracy Butler shout for help as one of the assailants held her by the hair and the other came from behind, armed with a knife.

The blade fell from one of the women's hands but she picked it up and began to stab Tracy Butler, at least six times. The witness ran for help as the victim fell to the ground before picking herself up and staggering towards a door.

"When they ran away, they jogged like girls," said Mr McCarthy.

Tracy Butler, fatally wounded, dragged herself along the road to a house before knocking on the door. She collapsed to the ground and as the door was answered, she could only mutter: "I can't breathe."

Phyllis Dumas, who owned the house, described how her brother opened the door of the house and the seventeen-year-old simply fell inside.

"She was covered in blood," said Mrs Dumas.

"Somebody help me," begged Tracy Butler. "I can't breathe."

She pleaded for water and they gave her a glass but it was clear to even the untrained eyes that her injuries were severe and that Tracy would be very lucky to survive the attack.

Once in garda custody, Deborah Hannon decided it was time to confess, putting her name to a written statement saying that she and Suzanne Reddan had planned the killing.

"Planned all the time," it read. "Suzanne and myself. We planned to kill Mark or Sharon or Tracy. I blamed them for killing my father. I kept thinking about my father. We planned it after the funeral. I had the Stanley blade that night. Suzanne had the knife down at Ballynanty."

The two women dressed deliberately in dark clothes that night. They knew Tracy Butler had not actually been involved in beating William Hannon to death, but she had been there in the mocking crowd and was guilty simply by association.

Her statement continued: "I told her: 'You're going down now like my father did.' I just kept thinking about my father. I think I used the Stanley knife on her face. I didn't think she was bad like."

They then threatened Tracy that her mother would be next.

"It happened very fast, we ran away. I wish it would all stop. I'm sick of it. I feel sorry now for all that has happened," Deborah Hannon said.

It was the only contrition she ever showed and when on trial, she pleaded not guilty to the murder of Tracy Butler.

Suzanne Reddan also made a statement to gardaí outlining how she had been in a relationship with William Hannon, after separating from her husband.

On the night Hannon was attacked on 2 July, she had stumbled upon the crime scene and saw people "smirking and sneering" as they walked away from the dying man. Tracy Butler had been at the scene and two days later, he had died in hospital. Suzanne Reddan admitted that she was "very bitter".

William Hannon had been a marked man since a fight had broken out at a disco a year previously, where he had been working as a bouncer. Gardaí had known that a number of people were "out to get him" but Willie Hannon feared nobody, saying "bullets won't kill me".

The incident had, somewhat familiarly in the city known as Stab City, led to a feud, slicing apart a number of families and friends, including Debbie Hannon and Tracy Butler, who had once been close pals.

On the night of the stabbing, Suzanne Reddan had taken a weapon with her "just in case". The previous night, she had also been out looking for Tracy. She had walked around the estates of Limerick, seeking her out, revenge at the forefront of her mind. On the fateful night, Reddan and Hannon were again out searching when they stumbled upon Tracy Butler walking towards them.

"As we came close," said Reddan, "Tracy started to smile and make faces at Deborah. We grabbed Tracy and pushed her across the road.

"Deborah and I beat her together. I got the knife and stabbed her in the chest area at least once. I heard Tracy Butler shout: 'Help me, help me.' I dropped the knife, I don't know if me or Deborah picked it up."

The memory of her dead lover had driven her to seek the ultimate revenge, she said: "Willie's face kept flashing in front of me and I was in a fit of temper."

The two killers fled the scene as a man approached, and they headed back to Deborah Hannon's house. As she washed the blood from her hands, guilt was already beginning to overcome her.

It was Deborah Hannon's mother Teresa who gave them up, outlining to gardaí the aftermath of the killing, when the two women came back to her house bloodied.

There was a knock at the door and Suzanne and Deborah came into the house. Teresa Hannon went to the kitchen where she saw the two women taking off their clothes. There was blood on their hands. They put their clothes in one bag and the knife in another. Teresa Hannon fainted. A man and a boy who were in the house took the items away to destroy them.

Most heartbreaking of all for Mrs Hannon was the fact that her daughter and Tracy Butler had once been the best of friends. "From the time they were in playschool until the death of my husband, those two girls were inseparable. They both left school after primary together and they looked out for each other. They were always fighting on each other's behalf."

But she knew there was little point in prolonging the inevitable and admitted to the detectives investigating the murder that her daughter had always been "wild".

She told Detective PJ Barry in her statement: "Deborah was always a bit wild. From the time she was a child, she was always getting up to things, or in prison for shoplifting and stealing. I just want to get the whole affair out of the way and get on with my life."

Prosecuting barrister Eamon Leahy admitted that it was a tragic case but the background to the crime could not be considered by the jury in reaching a verdict, he said.

"It is a tragic case," he said, "but tragic cases must have the law applied to them in the same way as any other case."

Deborah Hannon's defence lawyer said the accused was grief-stricken at the time and unable to think clearly. Statements taken by gardaí, he said, came about by the "oppressive" conduct of having interviewed them for too long, a claim later rejected when the women made an appeal against their conviction.

On behalf of Suzanne Reddan, barrister Patrick MacEntee repeated those claims, telling the jury that if there was any doubt in their minds about her intentions that night, they should find her guilty of only manslaughter.

In March of 1994, it took the jury of six men and six women six hours to find the two women guilty of the murder by a majority verdict. As the mandatory life sentence was handed down, Suzanne Reddan collapsed and cried. Deborah Hannon remained impassive as she began what would prove – by anybody's standard – an extremely short life sentence in the Irish prison system.

By 2002, the two women were already free from the Dóchas Centre at Mountjoy Prison, benefiting from the chronic overcrowding that has beset that small prison since the very first day it was opened.

Tracy Butler's mother was devastated on hearing the two women had already been released.

"I am heartbroken to the depths of my soul to hear my daughter's killers are out," she said. "My little girl lies in a cold grave and her murderers are free to live their lives. I am tormented by the death of my daughter. I am dead [since her murder] . . . and now I hear that justice has not been done," she told the *Irish Mirror*.

"Tracy might have been seventeen, but she only had the mentality of a thirteen-year-old. She was sent to a special school and was very innocent.

"I want her killers locked up and the key thrown away. I have written countless letters to the Department of Justice asking that they be kept in prison. They stabbed my daughter's little body countless times. I would put them in the same category as Myra Hindley.

"I'm in total shock. Everyone loved Tracy. People still talk to me about her when I meet them on the street. But all I have is a grave to go to. She was denied a future, the chance to fall in love and have children."

While Deborah Hannon again benefited from the apparently forgiving nature of the State in serving little more than eight years of what was supposed to be a life sentence, what was more infuriating for the Butler family is that she should have been in jail at the time of the killing.

Debbie Hannon was on temporary release at the time she carried out the murder, having been granted a series of ever-longer periods of freedom from a fourteen-month sentence she was serving for burglary.

When she knifed Tracy Butler to death, she was only seven months into that sentence. However, between 2 July and 17 July, when the murder took place, she had spent just a single night in jail.

Women by and large fare better in the Irish justice system compared to men, not least because of a lack of capacity in the only two women's prisons in the State, at Mountjoy and Limerick. Legislation also favours them, however, and in one famous sexual abuse case, a judge could only sentence a woman to seven years in prison under an antiquated law known as the Punishment of Incest Act. The mother had abused her six children over the course of six years, both physically and sexually. She had also left them malnourished and with lice in their hair. In passing sentence, the late Judge Miriam Reynolds explained: "Had this been a case of a male person being convicted – a much longer sentence would be allowed. A man convicted of incest can be jailed up to a maximum of a life sentence."

Comparing sentences served by female and male offenders is difficult, not least because the number of men committed to prison outnumbers women by eight to one. Available figures, however, for individuals serving life sentences show that a male "lifer" will spend on average seventeen years in jail. By comparison, the average sentence being served by a female for a life sentence between 2001 and 2007 stood at just eleven years.

Female offenders are also routinely granted early release, particularly so-called "drug mules" who carry sometimes large quantities of cocaine or other narcotics into Ireland. The "mules" benefit from particularly short sentences, because their crime is perceived as largely victimless and they are invariably forced to leave Ireland on release from prison.

In 2007, the number of women on what is known as reviewable temporary release (TR) stood at twenty-seven, or twenty-four per cent of the total female prison population. By comparison, just 126 men were free on TR, the equivalent of four per cent of all male prisoners in the system.

While Suzanne Reddan and Deborah Hannon may have only served a short sentence, in many cases female killers have not even made it to jail or have served remarkably short sentences.

In 1995, Norma Cotter shot her husband Gary dead, using a shotgun she had bought as a birthday present just a week earlier. Mrs Cotter was found guilty of murder in 1996 but the conviction was quashed and a retrial ordered. In 2003, she instead pleaded guilty to the lesser charge of manslaughter. It had been suggested that Gary Cotter had been violent towards his wife but no evidence was heard of the purported domestic abuse after the guilty plea was accepted.

Justice Michael Peart sentenced her to three and a half years in jail, saying there were "times when the court's punishment must be tempered with some mercy and compassion". Mrs Cotter, who the court heard had a young son and daughter to look after, walked free from court, having served the entirety of the eventual sentence whilst awaiting trial.

In October 2004, Dolores O'Neill was found guilty of the manslaughter of her husband Declan, whom she had beaten to death with a hammer. She had stabbed him twenty-one times and hit him with a blunt object twenty-six times – he was asleep at the time. She was given an eight-year jail sentence after claiming her husband was abusive and an alcoholic. In fact, the opposite appeared to be the truth.

In a statement read outside the court, Declan O'Neill's brother Brian refuted the allegations, saying: "What we heard in court was not our brother." Referring to the jury, he said: "You have made up your mind from what you heard in court. I will not fault you for your decision. The fault lies with the justice system in this country."

Another brother told how Declan O'Neill had kept a diary of his injuries, how his wife had hit him with a bottle, how she had rammed his car, how she phoned him up to forty times a day, and how she had stolen his medication and threatened to throw acid in his face.

The post-mortem had shown he was in good health and there was no evidence of excessive alcohol intake in his liver.

Dermot O'Neill said: "It is the family's view that he lived a life of quiet desperation. Regrettably, it was Declan's view that any steps he took were futile and tolerating the abuse was his only option."

In another even more complex case, in 2008 psychiatrist Dr Lynn Gibbs was found not guilty by reason of insanity of murdering her own daughter. Gibbs admitted drowning her daughter Ciara in the belief that the sixteen-year-old was suffering from anorexia and destined for a grim death from the eating disorder.

While no one would argue that Dr Gibbs was deeply ill at the time, a victim of a severe form of psychotic depression, other fathers had committed the same crime and received no such leniency.

Dr Gibbs was committed to the Central Mental Hospital for treatment and will likely be released from full-time medical care within a matter of years.

Another man, in an almost identical situation, was instead found guilty of murder and is currently serving a life sentence in prison. Somalian Yusif Ali Abdi suffered from severe paranoid delusions and believed gardaí were involved in a plot to get him.

In April 2001, he killed his young son Nathan in Clane, County Kildare, after banging his head against a wall three times. Two years later, he was found guilty of murder, despite the strong evidence of his mental state and the support of the child's mother.

If the eight or so years that Deborah Hannon and Suzanne Reddan spent behind bars seemed unreasonably light, the men responsible for the attack that killed William Hannon were perhaps even more fortunate.

In June 1994, three of them – Alan Duggan, Eric Ryan and John McGrath – pleaded guilty to assault occasioning actual bodily harm to Mr Hannon almost a year earlier. Their hearing was told that the State would not be proceeding with charges of murder.

Judge Feargus Flood imposed a sentence of three and a half years on Duggan and Ryan, whom he felt bore the brunt of the responsibility for what had happened. He suspended two years of their sentences and, taking into account the eleven months they had already spent in custody, the men were left with just a six-month sentence.

Judge Flood was even more forgiving when it came to sentencing John McGrath, handing down a two-year sentence with twelve months of it suspended. Based on the time already served in jail, McGrath walked from court a free man that day.

The trial had heard how, on the day of the incident, William Hannon had hit a woman and was then pursued by a gang of people, who had armed themselves with whatever implements or weapons they could find.

The row was merely the latest episode in the long-simmering feud which had begun at a disco five months earlier, gardaí involved in the investigation said.

Duggan carried a length of wood while Ryan was carrying a sewer rod. McGrath armed himself with a sheet of plywood. Who exactly hit Mr Hannon where was never clear and one of the men said he had only hit him across the chest. Medical evidence showed that the thirty-three-year-old had died from a fractured skull, caused by a direct blow to the side of his head.

As John McGrath walked free and Alan Duggan and Eric Ryan left to serve six months in jail, the sorry, vengeful saga of William Hannon and Tracy Butler came to an end.

19

David Bourke: Don't Kill Mammy

"I told dad not to kill my mum."

These are words that no seven-year-old child should ever have to utter; it sounds like something from a nightmare or a horror movie. But for David Bourke and Jean Gilbert's little boy, it was all too real.

It was 28 August 2007. The façade of what may have appeared at first glance to be normal suburban life in Dublin's leafy suburb of Castleknock was crumbling.

Bourke's world was falling apart. Jean was on the verge of leaving him. The forty-nine-year-old insurance administrator claimed he was not normally a violent man, just another husband trapped in a collapsing relationship. But his wife had just told him she had never loved him and that she wanted to separate after rekindling a relationship with English musician Robert Campion.

David Bourke had been through her diary and emails; the correspondence, texts and love letters were more befitting of two smitten teenagers. He "had his nose rubbed in it", the trial judge Barry White said.

His daughter had one day been playing around on the computer and had accidentally opened up her mother's email inbox.

"Daddy, what's this?" she asked.

David Bourke scrolled through the email message, a letter of love from his own wife to her new lover, Bob Campion.

"My dearest beautiful Bob you are to me extraordinarily beautiful. Handsome is such a cold, unfeeling word. I've always wanted you and it broke my heart not being able to be with you. My feelings for you are always so intense. I guess it was the depth of my feelings. I really want us both to live long healthy lives; I want us to be together for as long as possible in this lifetime. I can be so hard on myself sometimes and put myself under a lot of pressure and stress. I got so familiar with it I didn't know it was there, I didn't recognise it. It is gone now and I feel so alive and so free."

Bourke continued to read the email, unable to stop himself: he was "gutted", he had been "betrayed", and he was "hurt". "[I felt] threatened by this man coming into our relationship," he would later tell his own barrister. "He'd ripped our marriage apart and I felt so hurt, so devastated."

The email continued: "I loved the smell of that aftershave when combined with your skin. You talk about going back to Tokyo. It would be just amazing. It's changed a lot though. I would love to go back to the same hotel.

"I feel so close to you these days, sometimes I can almost see you and feel you are here with me. At other times, missing you becomes intolerable. I feel so close and connected to you. You and I feel so right together. My communication skills then were crap. Now I feel I can talk and talk to you forever. I won't burn your ears off.

"I am counting down these days till I see you. I just want to be in your arms again, feel you, smell you, kiss you, make love to you. I ache to be in your arms again, I really do. I have to go now; I have to get Alex from school. Once again, I've shed some tears in writing this email.

"Bob, I love you so much with my entire life I really do. I have never felt about anyone the way I feel about you. I didn't know love like this was possible but guess what it's f**king amazing. I love you so very much my beautiful man."

Robert Campion had also emailed in May 2007, a teenage love letter, which still had the power to bring David Bourke to tears even as it was read in court nearly two years later.

"Since receiving your letter I've written 100,000 or more words in my head. I know I'm tired and although this is the longest sentence, I'm going to write it before my head explodes. Everything you say is true. My body is aching and throbbing in the same way, but not just lust.

"I have the most profound respect for you and your struggle to overcome that. I am, as you know, by blood half-Italian, and as I age that half is becoming more the whole of my spirit."

The letter continued: "I digress; but I tell you, I want to be with you physically, not just spiritually. I want feisty. I want to feel you come all over me but, most of all, I want to be quiet with you; to sense you, to have your scent, to fold your clothes like I used to.

"To cook with you, grow old with you, to caress you gently, to curl up with you. To look after you when you have a chill or are poorly, to make you a cup of tea, to hold your hand, go for very long walks, to listen to music with you, to argue with you, to come inside you. To always make you feel safe. To stroke your spine. To run my finger through your hair. I want you to do what you want with me. I trust you, I love you, I respect you. All of the above is true and correct. My loins are soaking, so I change tack."

The husband, David Bourke, continued to read the words.

"Would I say what I'm feeling if I didn't feel it 100 per cent? No, of course not. She is provisional, you are true. You see, I am ruthless; I became world class by being ruthless. If I am happy so is the world. Valerie [his girlfriend] had her chance and blew it. Blew it because she had no balls. My feisty lady has the balls of a bull. I can see potential."

The letter starts to drift and become nonsensical but David Bourke must read on. How could any husband stop himself?

"As all women who have experienced me are aware, I'm bloody ruthless about exploitation. Until then, well I'm a f**king nightmare. If I'd been born in Sicily and not met this Buddhism, I would have been a don. Valerie is dead to me.

"I want my Jean. Yes, you're mine, not to control and manipulate, but to love like no man could ever love a woman more. Yes, I would love to have children with you but this is one thing time cannot change, but life is eternal and we will meet again and have loads of children.

"The most important thing now is to establish a life together. How this happens has to be handled with care because children are involved. One thing I firmly believe is that everyone has unique karma. Jean, I mean it, you can come here to me whenever you like.

"The truth is I've had no steady girlfriend since you. I've always said that not marrying you was the biggest mistake of my life, and because of that I didn't want anyone else. I felt the time was right to ignite the volcano, especially as you were shacked up with Monsieur Le Grumpy. I will never disappear from your life, but then love has never meant to me what it means now. I respect you Jean, in every sense, physically, spiritually and sexually. I would be fully honoured in the future if you would become my wife."

David Bourke went to put the letter down, before reading the last line: "Oh God, the most love that man could give a woman."

When Robert Campion first wrote a letter to Jean Gilbert in April 2007, he inadvertently began a chain of events that would ultimately lead to her death.

He told gardaí that they had first met on a Buddhist trip to Japan in 1986. For a year and a half after, they had kept up a long-distance relationship between his home in London and hers in Dublin.

After losing contact, Jean Gilbert penned a letter asking Bob to marry her.

"I got cold feet because I was a professional musician," he said.

In the years that followed, Jean Gilbert married David Bourke and Bob Campion had heard through friends that his old flame had settled down.

David Bourke was originally from Mullingar in County Westmeath and moved to Dublin in 1993 after getting a job with Hibernian Insurance. Within two years, he was married and in the years that followed he and Jean Gilbert would have three children together.

"I believed I had a very ordinary marriage, doing normal things with the kids, activities, visiting our families," he explained.

By 2007, Jean Gilbert had been married for twelve years. She appeared – at least to her neighbours – to have a happy marriage.

Campion decided he would try to resume contact and wrote Jean a letter. She replied and he responded, "testing the waters to see if she still had feelings". The waters of Ms Gilbert's marriage clearly ran shallow and, soon after, her contact with Bob Campion advanced to text and email messages.

David Bourke told the court how he knew something was wrong when his wife had asked to meet him in a pub one morning. Speaking through his tears, he said: "She told me she wanted to split up, split up with me and she didn't love me any more . . . and that she loved somebody else and that she'd never really loved me at all. That this man was the love of her life and she wanted to be with him and she was going to be with him. I was devastated. I can't tell you what it was like. I was so heartbroken. I suggested we go and get counselling but she wouldn't have it. She said: 'It's over, it's finished.' She said: 'I love this man and I want to be with him.' I had hope in my heart she might change her mind, she might see sense. I was just so devastated; I just went around shopping centres, wandering around, in a black mood, wandering around like a zombie."

By July 2007, the relationship had become a full-blown affair as Jean Gilbert visited her musician lover in England following a Buddhist trip to France.

A month later, she went back to Southampton, by which time Bob Campion had given up his job and flat and "planned to return to Ireland with Jean". On Sunday, 26 August, the couple boarded a ferry at Holyhead bound for Dublin Port, planning to start their new life together. Bob Campion booked into the Travelodge Hotel in Castleknock, just a short drive from Jean Gilbert's home, while he got himself on his feet.

David Bourke meanwhile was formulating plans to make up with his wife and told her he would do anything to keep her and the children. Any hopes he had of salvaging the marriage, though, were doomed to failure.

His wife had done nothing to hide the affair and had even brought her lover back to the family home.

"We went back into the house. [My daughter] came in the door first. She said: 'Daddy, there's a horrible smell of BO and smoke in here, do you get it?' I said: 'Yes, I do, it's terrible.' I went into the kitchen and saw there were two plates on the kitchen table, lying there with the remains of food, dinner. I thought, what the hell is going on here. I just couldn't understand it and thought maybe she'd brought him over. Just, unbelievable."

Jean denied that Campion had been in the house. "But I knew she was lying. I knew it was him. He was a heavy smoker. I felt very threatened. This man was here on my doorstep, in my house, having dinner with my wife. What was going to happen? Where was this going? I just felt like a cuckold."

That Monday, David Bourke texted a colleague: "She arrived back just as I was leaving to collect [my daughter]. Seems he came back with her. . . . Things got worse. We had a massive row. I told her there would be fisticuffs if he turned up in the house while I was there. I just hate her. I had to get out of the house or I would have killed her. I was that angry."

By Monday, Bob Campion was already on the hunt for a new job and a new flat. That evening, he met Jean Gilbert for a drink at the hotel in Castleknock. The forty-six year-old mother could never have imagined that she was only hours from death. She received a text from her husband: "Lies, lies, lies, you said you were going to visit your mother." Jean Gilbert returned home but was back at the hotel by 5.30 a.m., where she had sex with her lover.

She received one final text from David: "You're ruining my holiday."

Again, she returned home, a final fateful visit to her now inconsolable and enraged husband. Bourke was livid, demanding that his wife tell him whether she had taken their young son's phone and given it to her lover.

The couple's daughter – just ten at the time of the killing – later recalled to gardaí: "My dad came in. He was talking aggressively – like you do when you're cross."

David Bourke took a black-handled knife from his kitchen.

"Dad was standing in the doorway between the hall and the living room. He stepped towards her. He had a knife. I saw the knife when my dad pushed my mum over. She was pushed over the chair on her back. She tried to grab my dad's hand to stop him. He was trying to stab her."

"[Dad] said to me that she was gone to see her boyfriend. He was angry. He had an angry face on. My mum told dad she wanted a divorce. When he heard this for the first time, he said that he wanted to jump off a cliff. Mum and dad were fighting a lot since mum told dad she wanted a divorce. Mum told dad she wanted a divorce two months ago. Before that, they were fighting about little things. I don't know why she wanted a divorce."

Her brother, in his statement, recounted something no seven-year-old should ever have to witness: "Dad tried to put it [the knife] into mummy's tummy or head or something. I told dad not to kill my mum. He said 'stop it'. I can't remember where the knife went."

Jean Gilbert rolled on the ground. "Daddy thought my mum gave my phone to mum's boyfriend. My dad had the knife. He was trying to kill my mum. She said: 'I didn't do it, I didn't give the phone to my boyfriend.'

"Mum and dad were fighting about ten times before and then the knife thing happened. It never happened before."

Cold reality began to dawn on David Bourke and he rang the emergency services. Fireman Maurice McCann remembered how a man told him over the phone that he had attacked his wife and "stabbed her several times". The fireman could hear children crying in the background. David Bourke responded: "That's why somebody has to get here. I've three kids crying here. I'm not going to do anything else to her. She's still alive. The kids are in no danger. I love those kids."

By the time Garda Padraig Brennan arrived at the scene, Ms Gilbert's life was already slipping away from her. It was 10.30 a.m. when the Garda reached Laverna Downs and at James Connolly Memorial Hospital Jean Gilbert drew her last breath five hours later, dead at the age of forty-six.

By then, David Bourke was in custody. He had already admitted to Garda Brennan that he had "stabbed her three times". "He pointed to a knife with a black handle on the mantelpiece and said that was the knife he had stabbed her with," said Garda Brennan.

The motive was also becoming clear. Garda Brennan said: "[He'd] read the deceased's diary and that she was going to leave him and that is why he stabbed her."

The only question now remaining was whether David Bourke was guilty of murder or manslaughter. He said that he never intended to kill her.

"I went downstairs to the kitchen to put toast on. I got hold of the knife, went in to my wife and confronted her. I attacked her. I stabbed her," he confessed on the witness stand.

In a statement to gardaí, he said he had "lunged" at her when she was sitting in an armchair. He was "calling her names" as he stabbed her. He said: "My daughter came in, asking why did you kill her and what is going to happen to us now?"

"I loved her so much. I just couldn't bear it. I just couldn't take this. It was just too much. Oh God, God forgive me. Jean was the love of my life. She was the one I loved and I wanted to do everything possible to get this marriage to work."

As she lay dying on the floor of the family home, David Bourke made a desperate attempt to save her, giving her the "kiss of life".

He said: "I put some cushions under her, some tissues. I tried to make her comfortable. I called for an ambulance, the guards."

From the moment of the crime David Bourke never once denied it, never hid what he did, and never disguised his shame. Even as he stood in the witness box, fighting for his freedom, he sought forgiveness from the family of his late wife Jean. "Please can I say to the members of the court, to the jury, to the Gilbert family and my three beautiful children, from the bottom of my heart I'm deeply sorry for what happened. I truly am terribly sorry."

It may have been a portrait painted for the benefit of the judge and jury, however. Accounts after the trial of their doomed relationship were more complex, showing that the marriage had been on the verge of collapse for over ten years. Jean Gilbert had confided in friends that her husband had been abusive and Bourke had once smashed a large wedding portrait in front of one of their young children.

Not long before she died, one of her closest pals had confronted her and demanded she let go of whatever secrets she was keeping. Jean Gilbert broke down in tears, explaining how he controlled and manipulated her every move, how she was only entitled to a certain amount of money each week and that she was concerned about the way he was treating their children.

Her own family was forced to issue a statement in which they said the Jean Gilbert of the murder trial was simply a caricature of a loving woman who had been driven to the edge.

"It is with great regret and heavy hearts that we find it necessary to break our silence and speak for Jean," they said. "The past month has been very difficult for us to bear, with the great outpouring of sympathy for David Bourke, and the very unkind words used to describe Jean. David Bourke was not the man he claimed to be and Jean was certainly not the woman that David Bourke would like to portray.

"As we said after the verdict, we are unable to comment in detail on Jean's very sad marriage to David Bourke. Jean told her side of the story to her immediate family on 20 June 2007. That night she arrived at our parents' house, looking pale and extremely thin. She started by saying: 'This is the truth, the whole truth and nothing but the truth. I am fed up living a lie that everything is all right when it's not.'"

On 30 March 2009, David Bourke was found guilty of the murder of his wife Jean although, at the time of writing, his case was under appeal.

He will spend at least twelve years in jail, a fish out of water in a prison system more normally filled with gangland criminals, drug addicts and sexual offenders. When he finishes his sentence, he will be at least sixty years of age, but life – as he knew it – will never return to what it was before.

Meanwhile, Robert Campion, whose naïve letter of April 2007 began a chain of events nobody could possibly have foreseen, is back in England, a broken man.

He has forgiven David Bourke: "As difficult as it may be to understand, I forgive [him] . . . I very quickly forgave him for killing Jean."

Bourke's lawyers attempted to paint a picture of "a classless, ageing, half-Italian gigolo". But, according to Campion, their relationship meant much more than that. "We didn't have some kind of sordid affair," he said. "Jean did everything above board; she tried to save her marriage because she did love David. She gave him every opportunity but he just didn't listen.

"She told him she wanted a divorce. She asked him to leave the house but he refused. Finally, she agreed to let him have the house with the kids because she thought that was the best thing to do.

"This whole thing has been nothing but an orchestrated attack on Jean and on me."

He also portrayed a different version of events from that of the home-wrecker who deliberately set out to ruin a marriage.

Jean Gilbert had in fact instigated the first contact, he said, sending an email to commiserate on the death of his father. It was followed in Christmas of 2006 by a seasonal greeting card.

"I waited a couple of months but it niggled at me," he said. "I wondered how she was. I wanted to go visit Ireland and meet her family, I wanted to meet David and the kids. So I wrote to her and asked 'How are you?' She wrote straight back and started talking about her life and the kids. She never really mentioned David, which I thought was odd, and she was a bit negative in the first letter.

"I asked her what David did. I got this letter back saying: 'What does he do? He does this, sits in front of the telly all day long.' It was this tirade. I was genuinely shocked. She must have been really unhappy because I'd never heard her say a bad word about anyone.

"I sent her a letter saying that I needed her and wanted her. She didn't feel either of those things from David. He just did his nine-to-five work, came home and sat in front of the TV, cooked the dinner and that was it."

Bob Campion admitted that he had ultimately become the "catalyst" for the tragic events that would follow.

He said: "I'm not denying any responsibility because I was certainly the catalyst or accelerant to the situation, but my gut feeling is that it would have ended in tragedy one way or another. She would have had some sort of breakdown. She was that depressed."

Campion offered to meet with David Bourke and explain the situation to him but Jean Gilbert thought better of it.

He recalled: "She thought we might have fisticuffs. I told her I wasn't worried about that but she said that he might do it in front of the kids."

On the morning that she died, she returned to the Travelodge Hotel because the "atmosphere" in her own home had become intolerable.

Campion remembered: "There was a knock on my door at 5 a.m. I was completely surprised to see her but delighted of course. We made love, had breakfast and we did some [Buddhist] chanting for about an hour. Her little boy was starting school the next day so she wanted to go home and get him ready.

"We were also getting these mad texts from David about how she was ruining his holiday and I told her: 'Don't say anything to provoke him.' I had an idea of the place he was in. Obviously, I never expected what he actually did, but I thought he might give her a whack or something.

"She left and I was going to get on with my day. That was the last time I saw her," he said in the interview with the *Irish Mail on Sunday*, pointing out that he had not been paid to speak despite rumours to the contrary.

In a murder trial, everybody gets to have their own say, except the victim. The perpetrator can explain their actions, show remorse and create a version of events that in some way helps to exonerate themselves.

Those on the fringes like Bob Campion become collateral damage, victims of intimate words, emails or letters that were meant to be forever private.

But for Jean Gilbert, there was no chance to explain herself, no chance to justify the decisions she had made and the new life she had chosen for herself.

It was left to her brother Robert to give an emotional victim impact statement in which he tried to make real the "beautiful young lady who just loved life and lived life to the full".

He attempted to put in words what his niece and nephews had suffered: "The tragic loss of Jean, their mother, has had a profound impact on their lives.

"They each deeply miss her in their own special way. For [her eldest daughter] there will be no more shopping trips, no more trips to the coffee shop and no going to the hairdresser with Mum. [She] says: 'I'll never forget my Mum. She was the best, so nice. I loved you and miss you so much.'

"For [her eldest son]: 'I really miss her. I want my mum. I want to go home to my mum.'

"For [her youngest child], he misses his Mum's hot chocolate and watching her make his special dinner. One-to-one special time he had with his mum is now gone forever."

Jean Gilbert believed in reincarnation but this is scant consolation to her children, particularly the two who will forever bear witness to the day their beloved father took their mother's life.

Their names were withheld from court reports – and from this book – in an attempt to allow them some semblance of a normal life. But no passage of time will ever clear the memory of those horrible events for an eternally seven-year-old boy and ten-year-old girl.

20

Shay Wildes' Wild West

As Shay Wildes walked towards Joseph Cummins, he shouted at him: "Merry Christmas."

It was St Stephen's Day 2001. Wildes calmly raised his Bersa handgun and fired at Cummins from point-blank range. As the target slumped to the ground, already fatally wounded with a gaping hole in the back of his head, the assassin made certain to finish him off. He fired another two shots and any possibility of forty-eight-year-old Joseph Cummins surviving the attack was lost in those horrible moments.

Revenge was Wildes' motive that day – a murder carried out in direct reprisal for an alleged attempted sexual assault on his sister by Joseph Cummins more than a year previously. By September 2003, Wildes finally went on trial, accused of the St Stephen's Day murder of Joseph Cummins two years previously. He also faced charges of possessing a weapon and ammunition.

On the day of the murder, the two men had been drinking at the Dragon Inn in the sprawling Dublin suburb of Tallaght. A deadly grudge had been festering and Shay Wildes blamed Joseph Cummins, a father of five, for a violent attack on his sister eighteen months previously. Wildes' temper was rising and he had armed himself with a gun, which was stuffed inside his trousers.

One witness, Patrick O'Reilly, said that St Stephen's Day was permanently etched in his memory. He remembered how he was standing outside a taxi office on High Street in Tallaght when he saw a Peugeot car coming to a stop in front of him shortly before 8.00 p.m. A man stepped out of the passenger side and walked three paces towards Joseph Cummins, who had just left the Dragon Inn. O'Reilly watched in horror as the lone gunman shouted "Merry Christmas,'" before raising his weapon. "What I saw I'll never forget," he said, recalling the brutal assassination that took place just twenty yards from where he stood.

"He basically shot him in the back of the head as he shouted 'Merry Christmas'," said O'Reilly. "I said, 'Jesus: that man's been shot dead,' because I knew when he hit the ground he was dead." Still shaken from his experience that day, the witness continued his evidence: "I said, 'F**k me; I'm not going to let that happen in front of me.'"

When Wildes was finished, he walked back to the Peugeot car – "he didn't run" – and it drove away as Patrick O'Reilly made a mental note of the registration number. He walked inside the taxi office and shouted out the number to the controller there. As he stepped outside again, the car had already made good its escape. "Base control gave me a pen and paper and I wrote down the registration number of the car and the make," O'Reilly explained.

Gardaí matched the registration of the vehicle to Valerie Reid, Shay Wildes' partner, who owned a house at Corbally Park off the Blessington Road in Tallaght. A team of armed detectives swooped that night, less than three hours after the murder had taken place, finding an array of weaponry in the house. A .22 calibre semi-automatic handgun was found just lying on the couch in the house while loose bullets, a .22 magazine with one round inside and a baseball cap were sitting beside it. Further searches yielded five more .38 calibre bullets that were discovered in a plastic bag above a cupboard in the kitchen.

Detectives took Wildes into custody, where he admitted that the gun they had found had been used to commit the murder. At one stage, gardaí showed him the semi-automatic handgun and asked him if he had seen it before.

"Yes, that's the gun you found at my home," he said. "It's the gun I used to shoot Joe Cummins."

Wildes admitted the attack, saying that Joseph Cummins had tried to sexually assault his sister Catherine and had hit her with a crowbar. The alleged attack had never been reported to gardaí, however.

"She lost a lot of blood," claimed Wildes.

Shay Wildes originally said that he had kept the gun in the top of his trousers for his own protection and had shot Cummins not long after they had left the Dragon Inn, where they had by happenstance been drinking separately.

"I was talking to a fella beside me and I was drunk and told him [the] situation. And he says . . . he could get me something."

Detective Garda John Stack quizzed him further.

"Did you ask him could he get you a weapon?"

"No," said Wildes.

"Did he offer to get you a weapon?"

"Yep."

"Did you discuss money?" asked the garda.

"Yeah, when he offered it."

"Did you ask him what exactly you were going to get for your £200?"

"He just said that he would get me a weapon," said Wildes.

"I was full of drink," explained Wildes. "It just happened. I went blank after that. It was on me mind. I was going to get him back for what he done . . . I wished to get revenge, yeah."

Quizzed as to how many shots he had fired, he answered: "I don't know." Asked where he had shot him, he replied: "As far as I know, in the head."

After the murder, Wildes admitted he had moved on to another hotel where he continued drinking before returning home a couple of hours later.

Gardaí pressed him about why he had waited so long before exacting his revenge but Shay Wildes insisted that Joseph Cummins had gone "missing" in the immediate aftermath of the alleged assault.

"Was it always in your mind to do him harm of some description?" asked the interrogating garda. "Yes, like any brother would," he said in statements made in custody that he would later deny had ever been made.

Gardaí also tried to determine where Wildes had come across the pistol, giving him the names of two suspects that they believed had provided him with the weapon for a purchase price of €200.

"The man that gave me the gun showed me how to use it" was all he would say, unwilling to offer up any further information and refusing to name the person who had driven the vehicle that night.

In the end, Wildes had little chance of a reversal in his trial. Statements made to gardaí had been recorded and those recordings were shown to jurors, some of the first videotaped interviews ever used in an Irish courtroom.

On 24 September 2003, Shay Wildes – who was then thirty-five – was found guilty of the murder of Joseph Cummins. He was also found guilty on the firearm possession charges and was handed down two life sentences for his crimes. On two counts of possessing ammunition, he was given sentences of ten and five years respectively.

Trial judge Paul Carney said: "The unfortunate Joseph Cummins was executed on High Street, Tallaght, on December 26, 2001." He paid tribute to the brave witness who had not only remembered the number plate but had dared to give evidence despite being "severely traumatised" by what had happened.

After the guilty verdict, Joseph Cummins' partner Martina Murphy – who was also a cousin of Shay Wildes – issued a statement of just four words: "I hope he rots."

Her partner Joseph had been killed "instantly", the murder trial heard, from a "laceration of the brain stem due to a single bullet wound to the back of the head".

Gardaí walked from court somewhat contented. Any day a dangerous man like Shay Wildes is taken off the streets is a victory for the detectives who face a daunting task in proving guilt in any gun murder.

Conviction rates for murders carried out with firearms run very low in Ireland, fuelled by the anonymity a gun can offer and a widespread anxiety among witnesses about coming forward for fear of reprisals. In the six years leading up to 2008, the rate of conviction for gun crime in the Republic stood at just seventeen per cent, a poor return by any standards.

The Joseph Cummins case, however, had none of the usual hallmarks that make solving a gun murder so difficult. Shay Wildes' actions were on the spur of the moment and there was a clear motive of revenge. He had been careless, taking his chance whilst drunk and making little effort to disguise either himself or the getaway car. Things could easily have been so different. One garda speculated that had Shay Wildes worn a mask and obscured the number plates of his car, he could well be a free man today. They might never have arrested him that night and by the time he was eventually in custody, it would probably not have been as easy to extract a confession.

The bravery of Patrick O'Reilly, the state's chief witness, was also astonishing. Here was a man not prepared to sit back and allow the pall of fear engendered by crime to get the better of him. His information and instincts in noting down the registration plate led gardaí directly to Shay Wildes and the murder weapon.

POOLBEG WISHES TO
THANK YOU

for buying a Poolbeg book and will give you
20% OFF (and free postage*)
on any book bought on our website
www.poolbeg.com

Select the book(s) you wish to buy
and click to checkout.

Then click on the 'Add a Coupon' button
(located under 'Checkout') and enter
this coupon code

  # CAUEA15165

POOLBEG   (Not valid with any other offer!)   POOLBEG

WHY NOT JOIN OUR MAILING LIST
@ www.poolbeg.com and get some
fantastic offers on Poolbeg books

*See website for details

MORE BLOODY WOMEN

Ireland's Most Dangerous Females

DAVID M. KIELY

From the author of *Bloody Women* and *Deadlier than the Male*, seventeen more cases of death, violence and intrigue at the hands of some of Ireland's most notorious women ...

There has been a huge increase in violent deaths in Ireland in recent years. While men are more often the killers, there has been a rise in the number of murders committed by women. There is no single reason for this; some of the women featured in *More Bloody Women* killed for love gone wrong; some as revenge; some in the heat of the moment; some in cold blood. For some women, it was just business.

Among the infamous cases in this book are the "Black Widow", Catherine Nevin, who set up her husband's murder in Jack White's Inn; Linda and Charlotte Mulhall, the "Scissor Sisters", who killed and dismembered their mother's violent boyfriend before dumping the remains in a canal; Sharon Collins, who tried to hire a professional assassin to kill her partner; Kelly Noble, who stabbed a friend to death outside a supermarket, and whose own mother was already in prison for killing Kelly's father; and Lynn Gibbs, who tragically drowned her daughter in a bath because she believed the girl was suffering from anorexia.

David Kiely looks at all of these cases in forensic detail. He also delves into the fascination we have with women killers, and the media circus that surrounds every murder trial involving a woman. *More Bloody Women* is a chilling book that will shock and disturb.

978-1-84223-411-2